WORLD
WAR TWO
Voices From Wales

About the Book

"This fantastic collection is a testimony of service, sacrifice, valour, duty, and the sheer bloody-minded grit and determination that embodies the Welsh spirit. The generation that served in the Second World War are leaving us now, their numbers dwindling, but this priceless collection will keep their memory and their stories alive."

James Phillips, Veterans' Commissioner for Wales

"This enjoyable book ensures that the sacrifices and stories of Wales's greatest generation will never be forgotten."

Britain at War Magazine

"This book brings us the words of people who were at the places and battles which have gone down in history. The Battle of Britain. Dunkirk. El Alamein. D-Day. Arnhem. Nagasaki… These are the words of witnesses to history which should not be forgotten."

Dame Siân Philips

A donation from every book sold goes to Age Cymru Dyfed's Veterans' Archive, to help fund the collection of veterans' stories.

WORLD WAR TWO

Voices From Wales

HISTORY AS TOLD BY MEMBERS OF OUR 'GREATEST GENERATION'

HUGH MORGAN & G J LEWIS

*Dedicated to all those who served or
lost their lives in the fight against fascism
during World War Two*

First impression: 2025

© Copyright Hugh Morgan, G J Lewis and Y Lolfa Cyf., 2025

The publishers wish to acknowledge
the support of the Books Council of Wales.

Cover design: Sion Ilar

Front cover image: West Wales Veterans' Archive
(with thanks to Dennis Tidswell)

Back cover images: West Wales Veterans' Archive
(with thanks to Mary Bott) [left]; Hugh Morgan [right]

Other photos: © Hugh Morgan & G J Lewis,
unless otherwise stated

ISBN: 978-1-912631-55-1

Published and printed in Wales
on paper from well-maintained forests by
Y Lolfa Cyf., Talybont, Ceredigion SY24 5HE
website www.ylolfa.com
e-mail ylolfa@ylolfa.com
tel 01970 832 304

Contents

Foreword

ONE OF MY very earliest memories is of being wrapped in a blanket and carried into the garden by my mother to watch, mesmerised, as Swansea burned during the 'Three Night Blitz'.

It was a horrible and confusing sight. My mother could read her newspaper by the light of the flames, although Swansea was nine miles away.

My father was the village policeman, and he received training in how to defuse bombs and shoot a rifle. Everyone feared that the Nazis would cross the English Channel and come up the valley. Even the God-fearing chapel deacon was ready to fight.

I have often wondered about the other stories from Wales. About the people who were in the heart of the bombing of Swansea and Cardiff. About young people who, unlike me, did not have a safe home, but perhaps found refuge in Wales.

And about the many men and women from Wales who risked – and often gave – their lives in all corners of the world in this global war.

It is wonderful to see so many of their stories in *World War Two: Voices from Wales*. This book brings us the words of people who were at the places and battles which have gone down in history. The Battle of Britain. Dunkirk. El Alamein. D-Day. Arnhem. Nagasaki.

The power of their words allows us to look afresh at these momentous events and to reconsider them from the point of view of the ordinary person thrown into extraordinary circumstances.

Many people who have spoken to the authors of this book are now no longer with us. And one day soon, all the members of that wartime generation will be gone. That is why these are such important stories to record. These are the words of witnesses to history which should not be forgotten. Because, sadly, war always seems to be with us.

With its dozens of interviews, gathered over many years, *World War Two: Voices from Wales* ensures that even when the people who lived through these world-changing events are no longer with us, their stories – and the many lessons we can learn from them – shall live on.

> At the going down of the sun and in the morning,
> We will remember them.
> *Pan elo'r haul i lawr, ac ar wawr y bore,*
> *Ni â'u cofiwn hwy.*

Dame Siân Phillips,
March 2025

Preface

As THE PASSING of time forces us to say our final goodbyes to the last of the 'Greatest Generation' who lived through World War Two, not just in Wales but also further afield, it is vitally important that we record their personal stories, allowing their voices to be heard and enabling succeeding generations to learn from their experience of the most destructive war in humankind's history.

We have collected the first-hand accounts published here over more than three decades. They are the stories of the World War Two generation, garnered from interviews and written correspondence, often resulting in close and long-term friendships. Having met and recorded the life stories of men and women from many nations, on both sides of the conflict, we were both keen to publish a book commemorating those who were born or lived in Wales.

Our main difficulty was working out what was most important to include and what we could afford to exclude – for every personal story had value, not just as military history but as social history, with stories of communities, of family, of friendships and even of finding love. As well as a Welsh context, we aimed – where possible – to include men and women whose stories covered the whole of the war, allowing the reader to follow them through from the fears and uncertainty which came with the outbreak of hostilities to the celebrations and often equal uncertainty which arrived with war's end.

Many were just children when the war started, and their journey often began through the civil defence forces as fire watchers, messengers, first aiders, perhaps moving into the

Home Guard, and then on to the Women's Land Army, the RAF, Royal Navy, British Army and Special Forces. Others came to Wales from Europe in 1939 as very young children, seeking refuge from Nazi persecution.

These stories from Wales include those who put their lives on the line and repeatedly faced death, from France in 1940, to surviving the terrors of the Blitz in Pembroke Dock, Cardiff and Swansea. Baling out of planes which had been turned into fireballs at 20,000 feet over occupied territory, to evasion, interrogation and the brutality of incarceration in prison camps in German territory and the Far East. Taking part in immensely perilous Arctic and Atlantic convoys. Then of course, there were many from Wales who took part in the invasions of Sicily, mainland Italy, Normandy or in the war in the Pacific, Burma or India. At the end of the war, there were those who witnessed the aftermath of the surrender of Japan.

Sadly, many of those whose stories are contained in this book are no longer with us – a fact that made our mission to record their memories all the more essential and poignant. A few remain, although most are now around a century old. It has been an absolute privilege and pleasure to have met each and every one of them, and we thank them all for sharing with us their stories from this most desperate period in our nation's history.

One final point: the World War Two generation featured in this book were once young people who lived through an era in which personality-driven populism and authoritarianism, always male-led, brought about a marginalisation of whole races and populations, and set the world against itself. Countries were invaded and subjugated, with millions of innocent lives lost. A world truly at war. Our Voices of World War Two contained in this book witnessed the cost of this hatred, of the rush to violence. 80 years on, as the world seems to be lurching once again into a similar kind of rhetoric and division, we should take heed of the lessons learned by our World War Two generation as the warning signs – ignored by many in the 1930s – once again flicker red.

To learn from history is to understand the lives of those who were there. We record and reflect on the 'World War Two: Voices from Wales' because we will never see their like again, and because they have so much to say which is of value to us, both now and in the future.

Acknowledgements

OUR MAIN THANKS go to those whose stories have been drawn upon in the book: Charles Ackerman, Nick Archdale, Charlie Barnes, Florence Bird, Tony Bird, Mary Bott MBE, Neville Bowen, John Brock, Emil Clade, Renate Collins BEM, Don Davies, Syd Daw, George Duffee, A J C 'Bing' Eagles, Hugh Edwards, Doug Evans, Eric Evans, John Evans, Mary Griffiths, Duncan Hilling, Glyn James, Hugh 'Jimmy' James, Stewart Johnson, Ron Jones, Trevor Jones, Elaine Kidwell, Enid Lewis, Iori Lewis, Oliver Lindsay, Ken Lloyd, Adelaide Martin, John Martin, Jean McKay, Maldwyn Mills, Kemys Morgan, Ted Owens, Vernon Parry, Richard Pelzer, Pauline Penrose, Gordon Prime, Reg Pyatt, Stanley Roberts, Margaret Samuel, Wyndham Scourfield, Fred Seal, Dame Stephanie Shirley CH, Les Spence, Idwal Symonds, Archie Thomas, Dennis Tidswell. Also, to all of their families, friends or carers who have helped us collect their stories.

We have been grateful for support from Ken Burton, Neil Davies, Owen Dobson, Michael Evans, Ian Gane, Caroline Hayley, Dinah Jones, Sheila McDaid, Jeremy Spence, Pam Spurway and Martin Wade. Thanks to Nigel Davies, relative of George Roberts, for access to George's wartime documents, and to John Evans and Marie Neige-Hadfield for their assistance in the story of John's late aunt, WAAF Dorothy Evans from Tal-y-bont, who was killed in 1944.

We'd also like to express our appreciation to Age Cymru Dyfed's West Wales Veterans' Archive, held online on People's Collection Wales, National Library of Wales, a superb digital resource of veterans' stories, from the First and Second

World Wars to more recent conflicts. Some other interviews have previously appeared in ITV Wales/Age Cymru Dyfed's *Greatest Generation* film (screened 7 June 2022); ITV Wales' *Wings Over Wales*; *From Java to Nagasaki* by Les Spence; *Combat Kill* by Hugh Morgan and Jurgen Seibel; and *Airman Missing* by Greg Lewis: thank you to those who have given permission for us to reproduce them here.

Special thanks also to Carolyn Hodges, our editor, and the rest of the team at Y Lolfa.

Finally, we would like to thank Dame Siân Phillips for supporting this book with her wonderful foreword.

Hugh Morgan & G J Lewis,
April 2025

Prologue: The Road to War

WALES, LIKE EVERY nation involved in the First World War, knew only too well the pain and suffering caused by the industrial-scale destruction resulting from twentieth-century warfare. More than a quarter of a million Welshmen and women had been involved in that conflict in some way; more than 30,000 had died. For thousands of those who served, the scars – mental and physical – remained years later. Families still ached with their loss. So during the 1930s, fears of another war, coming so quickly after the last, naturally filled many with worry and even terror. Technological advances in the air would mean that the bombing of cities and towns was almost certain to lead to high numbers of civilian casualties. This time, Welsh civilians would feel like they were in the front line.

On 30 September 1938, the Munich Agreement between Britain and Germany was greeted with great relief. As the headlines celebrated 'Peace in our Time', the *South Wales Echo* described people in the streets waving their newspapers and shouting, "There isn't going to be any war!" In the spirit of international brotherhood that followed, the flags of many nations flew above Cardiff's City Hall – among them, the Nazi swastika. It stayed aloft only for a short time following complaints from councillors who sensed that Herr Hitler was neither to be lauded nor trusted. How right they were to be proven, and in a very short time too.

The dreams of peace grew cloudy with fears of war in March 1939, when Hitler sent his armies into the parts of Czechoslovakia he did not yet occupy. That spring saw the first big surge of young men volunteering for military service.

According to historian Dennis Morgan, Cardiff's Territorial Army Office stayed open for 24 hours straight at one point to deal with the new applicants standing outside in Queen Street. The Westminster government began the grim task of estimating how many lives might be lost in air raids and how it might house the families made homeless by bombing.

In August, French aircraft carried out a mock air raid on Cardiff to give Fighter Command an idea of how it might defend the city. Welsh troops were seen on the beach at Barry Island, filling sandbags, as parents and children looked on. Trenches, which could be covered with corrugated iron sheets, were dug in the more heavily populated areas of Wales. In Abergavenny, an air raid siren test, carried out without informing the population, sent a cold shiver down spines.

Then on Friday, 1 September 1939, Hitler invaded Poland. A feeling of deep unease rose in the pit of the stomach of those already in uniform. Britain and France sent Germany an ultimatum, demanding Hitler withdraw his armies from Poland. Europe and the rest of the world waited on the dictator's reply. It was a weekend of sunshine in Wales, but the sun was to herald a war that would touch virtually every family in the nation in some way.

At dawn on Sunday, 3 September, a Sunderland flying boat stationed at RAF Pembroke Dock took off from the waters of Milford Haven and embarked on what was to be the first wartime operational patrol of Britain's coastline. The sheltered, deep waters of the haven, by 1943 the largest flying boat station in the world, would become a vitally important base for both the Royal Navy and RAF Coastal Command in the coming years.

Radio was the world's mass communicator: it was both where comedians made their names and where history was announced. The sets came in a variety of shapes and sizes, housed in polished wooden cases, with two, three or even four knobs. Their dials displayed a wide range of British and Continental stations, listing cities which sounded exotic but which would soon become synonymous with battles.

At 11.15 a.m. that morning, families gathered round the wireless set in homes the length and breadth of Wales. Some – especially the youth – were eager with anticipation to hear the news but others, who perhaps had personally witnessed the devasting impact wrought by Mons, the Somme, Passchendaele and Gallipoli, could not hide their increasing anxiety about another war against the growing military might of Germany.

A cut-glass BBC accent crackled through the airwaves: "This is London. You will now hear a statement by the Prime Minister."

The next voice belonged to Neville Chamberlain:

I am speaking to you from the Cabinet Room of 10 Downing Street. This morning, the British Ambassador in Berlin handed the German government a final note, stating that unless we heard from them by 11 o'clock that they were prepared at once to withdraw their troops from Poland, a state of war would exist between us. I have to tell you now that no such undertaking has been received, and that consequently this country is at war with Germany.

What followed were six years which would affect the lives of millions, cause human suffering on an unprecedented scale, and shape the world in which we live today.

1

A Call to Arms

"I was only 14 years old, but my mother said,
'Oh, it'll all be over by…' Little did she realise
herself what was to come!"

SYD DAW

Sunday, 3 September 1939

From his home in Nannerch, Flintshire, Nick Archdale looked
back to that fateful day on which war was declared:

> I can remember sitting and listening to Chamberlain
> announcing in Parliament that we were at war and my father
> saying he was going straight back in. He'd been in the first
> war, of course, and he went straight back to his regiment to
> join up again.
>
> I was at school and all we wanted to do was to be old
> enough to join up before the war was over, and to take part.

This was a story very familiar to many families in Wales.
Dennis Tidswell remembered:

> I had been brought up in a small village called Gendros, about
> three miles outside of Swansea. My father was a member of
> the Swansea Police Force. He served during the First World
> War – was in the Grenadier Guards, and rose through the
> ranks, and at the end of that war was granted a commission.

In the garden of their house, Arfyn, in Whitland, Great Western Railway station master Stanley Morgan and his 16-year-old son Ted (by 1943 himself a pilot in the RAF) immediately constructed their Anderson shelter. Over 1.5 million of these corrugated steel constructs, each to be covered with one foot of garden earth, had been issued to families by 3 September 1939. The family's income determined whether these were received free of charge or for a £7 fee. They were named after Home Secretary Sir John Anderson, who had been given responsibility for preparing Britain to withstand aerial bombing by the German air force, the Luftwaffe.

For Stanley and his wife Edith, thoughts of the devastation caused to families by World War One grew ominously in their minds. Their eldest son, Kemys, was already serving in the RAF as a member of aircrew and their eldest daughter Chrissie was training as a nurse.

But there were plenty confidently declaring a view that the coming war would soon be over. Teenager Syd Daw recalled Chamberlain's announcement of war:

> I was in St Alban's Church [in Splott, Cardiff] on that Sunday morning, 3 September. We came out of Mass and went to Splott Park. It frightened me to wonder what was going on when we heard. I was a child, I was only 14 years old, but my mother said, 'Oh, it'll all be over by…' Little did she realise herself what was to come!

But just as at the start of World War One, Chamberlain's declaration of war inspired young people to volunteer with the Armed Forces. In Goodwick, John Evans recalled:

> My brother Doug and I were working for my uncle in Swansea, in his builder's merchant business. When war broke out, I was just the age to go. I had instructions to register in Swansea. I joined the Army, later transferring to the RAF.

There could be frustration for those too young to join up. Born in Neyland before moving to Pembroke Dock, where his father ran the Olive Bar public house in Pembroke Street, Ted Owens was champing at the bit to take on the Nazis.

When [war] started, I was just turned 15 and straight away I wanted a gun, so I tried to join the Home Guard with my brother. They gave him a rifle because he was two years older, and I was so annoyed over that. I thought, 'I won't be beat,' and I joined the fire brigade.

Though I couldn't read or write, they took me on as a messenger boy. [But] I was so ashamed when they were asking me to take messages, I was telling little white lies, like I fell over off my bike and I hurt my arm and things like that. But the girls that were in the telephone room, they took charge and because I used to stay in that room with the telephone girls at night, unless there was an alarm on, they took me under their wing and taught me to read and write.

Dennis Tidswell was set on becoming a pilot, but there was just one seemingly insurmountable problem, for at just 17 years and 2 months, he was almost a year too young.

My favourite hobbies were photography and radio. My father was a keen amateur radio enthusiast and in the early 1930s we were just coming out of the crystal set and moving into wireless sets made with thermionic valves. So he had taught me how to build a wireless set, and one day I took it into my head that I would like to join the Royal Air Force. Another one of my hobbies was aero-modelling and flying model aeroplanes. One particular morning I go to the RAF Recruiting Office at the bottom of Page Street in Swansea, and sat in front of this group of RAF officers...

"What age are you, my boy?"

"I'm 17."

"Well, come back when you're 18."

I went past the Sergeant at the door at the entrance. He said, "You're 18 next week, aren't you, boy?"

I said, "No, no, it's next July."

"You're 18 next week – aren't you, boy?"

I got the message… and I came back two or three weeks later and found myself sitting in front of this group of RAF officers at the Recruitment Centre. They look at your educational background, and then ask about your pastimes and hobbies. When I mentioned that I was interested in wireless, and could build a wireless set, they cottoned onto that one, and we talked very much about that. Well, I very much wanted to train as a pilot, that was the whole point of going in there, to learn to fly and to be a pilot. But they said I should join now as a radio operator, and then at some later date I could quite easily re-muster, and train as a pilot. But things didn't quite turn out that way.

Iori Lewis, who was 20, had no idea where the war would eventually take him. But it started quietly enough:

I was the depot manager in Cardigan of the Shell British Petroleum Company and in June 1939, as my friends were joining the TAs [Territorial Army], I decided to join 407 Battery, which was part of the 146 Field Regiment of the Pembroke & Cardiganshire Yeomanry.

I wanted to get away because it was an adventure, you know: to get out of the rut of the day-to-day tasks you were doing. And I was sort of looking forward to some adventure, to getting away from my hometown.

We moved from Cardigan on 28 December 1939 with a rumour that we were going to France, but we landed up in Llandudno for three months on coastal defence. Then we moved around the Midlands – training, of course; guarding factories; doing exercises in Salisbury Plain.

The Welsh sporting community wanted to play their part in the battle to come. In large groups, players joined a Territorial Army unit known as the 77th Heavy Anti-Aircraft Regiment, tasked with providing anti-aircraft defences for Cardiff, Newport and Barry. These included Glamorgan cricketers and most of the pre-war Cardiff RFC team, including Wilf Wooller and Les Spence, who had recently captained the side. The unit also included Hugh Edwards, who had been born in Blaenclydach but brought up by an uncle and aunt in Cardiff.

> Things were beginning to look a bit bleak for us then, and I got called up into the services before the beginning of the war. There were three batteries in the 77th. There was 241, which was in Caerphilly, 239 was in the Rhondda – Ystrad Mynach – and I joined the Cardiff group: the 240.
>
> The first activities that we had was when our unit was brought into Newport, as defence. But it was not just defence of Newport – we had sight of Bristol and aeroplanes going across to the Midlands and Liverpool. We were in their line.

Several of Wales' sports stars would not return from the war. Among them was Cardiff City goalkeeper John 'Jackie' Pritchard, who like Hugh had joined the 77th; he died in the Far East. Pontypridd-born Haydn Dackins, once of Swansea Town, lost his life during the Allied invasion of Sicily in 1943. Former Colwyn Bay player Albert Potter became an air raid warden and died during the Exeter Blitz. Newport-born John Evans, of Wales and the Barbarians, joined the Parachute Regiment and was fatally shot by a sniper in Tunisia in 1943.

Both Wrexham's goalkeeper Billy Bryan, who had joined the club at the start of the 1939/40 season, and one of Wales' greatest sporting all-rounders, Glamorgan cricket captain, England Test player and Wales rugby and hockey International Maurice Turnbull, were killed in Normandy in 1944.

2

Evacuation from France

"And of course, that's when the whole
thing blew up, you see? Horrific. There was
nothing we could do about it."
GLYN JAMES

THE ALLIES WAITED and waited for a German advance into
the west of Europe. The British Expeditionary Force (BEF),
which grew to 390,000 men over the harsh winter of 1939–
1940, deployed alongside the troops of its allies in France
and Belgium, but little happened. The Allies dug in along the
French border, facing the enemy, but there was no fighting.
This period of inaction and anticipation became known as
the 'Phoney War'.

In Llechryd, Ceredigion, just before her 100th birthday,
Pauline Penrose recalled those early days of the war.

My father joined the RAF, not as a young man. He was a
cabinetmaker and had been in the First World War, as a
Sergeant. He was in the British Expeditionary Force [in the
Reserve], which was sent over there [to France], and he said,
strangely enough there were men over there fixing Rolls-
Royce engines to German planes and when war was declared
they had to finish it, in order to be paid. Strange, isn't it,
really?

The autumn of 1939 turned into the bitterly cold winter of 1939–40. Sergeant Kemys Morgan, posted to 105 Squadron, arrived at the grass airfield in Villeneuve-les-Vertus, south of Reims:

> I was billeted with a French family in the village of Villeneuve. We had a crew of three on the [Fairey] Battles, consisting of pilot, observer/bomb-aimer and gunner.

In early April 1940, German forces invaded Denmark and Norway and then, in May, they began their *Blitzkrieg* ('lightning war') to conquer the Netherlands, Belgium and Luxembourg. By advancing through the heavily forested Ardennes, the Germans were able to swing south towards Sedan and avoid France's main defensive wall, the Maginot Line.

Glyn James of Kinmel Bay had joined the Royal Army Service Corps (RASC) at the outbreak of war and quickly found himself in France, where – as he spoke fluent French – he often worked as a liaison with local civilians and French forces. His unit was based in Œuilly near Épernay when, on 10 May 1940, the Germans struck west.

> When the balloon went up and Jerry burst through the Maginot Line, everything was a panic. All the roads were absolutely packed and everybody was trying to get away before the German onrush. All communications between us and HQ were torn down, so we had no way of communicating with anybody.

Glyn's unit were advised by a French officer to head to Dunkirk in the hope of being evacuated to England, and had just passed Reims when they had to stop at the head of a valley.

> We were looking down the valley towards Berry-au-Bac aerodrome and we could see it was being bombed. We could

see the German planes swooping down and unloading their bombs. So we waited until the bombing subsided.

The raid by twin-engine Heinkel He 111 bombers left the grass airfield, home to 142 Squadron, pockmarked by bomb craters, which the RASC men tried to help the RAF to repair.

We started to dig for earth to fill in the bomb craters so the planes could take off. But everywhere we were digging, we were digging up the bones of soldiers from the First World War. This chap was bringing buttons to me from the bodies. And as we were talking, we looked up and we could see a perfect formation of Jerry bombers come in towards the airport again, and we could see the bombs leaving the aircraft to bomb us. So we started to run, of course, and take shelter before they bombed the aircraft.

142 Squadron was one of the ten Fairey Battle squadrons serving with the 'Advanced Air Striking Force' in France. Another, 105 Squadron at Villeneuve-les-Vertus, had two Welsh boys serving as Air Observers: 28-year-old Sergeant Arthur 'Taffy' Morgan from 6 Union St, Ammanford, who had just returned to the squadron from a period of leave, and 20-year-old Kemys Morgan from Whitland.

In 2024, Ken Burton from Ammanford remembered:

Arthur and my father, George Burton, were very good friends, being members of the All Saints choir and school friends. They only lived a few hundred yards apart and played cricket on the school field at the rear of their homes.

Kemys Morgan recounted:

Our bombing sorties were only short trips and often at quite low level. Navigation wasn't really needed for these short trips, so the ground crews had fixed up, Heath-Robinson-like, a Vickers machine gun in the belly of the aircraft, which was designed to protect us from attacks underneath. Unfortunately for me, as the observer/bomb-aimer, I then became an additional gunner – which meant me dangling by a monkey chain, exposed underneath and outside of the aircraft, firing at will against the attacks of the German fighters. It was very hairy!

Another thing I learned to do quite quickly in France was to sit on a piece of lead whilst flying sorties, in order to give some protection to my vitals. You didn't want married life being curtailed even before it had a chance to start! This was something I did on every mission I flew for the rest of the war.

It was a hopeless situation. Crews went out time and again in the first two weeks in May 1940, facing almost certain death. Every time the low-flying Battles tried to destroy the pontoon bridges over the River Meuse, they were met by blankets of withering anti-aircraft fire, which subsided only when marauding German Messerschmitt Bf 109s, whose experienced pilots had already honed their combat skills in Poland and before that in Spain, wreaked their murderous havoc on the slow, vulnerable Battles.

It was the ultimate demonstration of selfless courage and losses were shockingly high. Arthur Morgan was a member of Flying Officer Wall's crew, and behind him sat Leading Aircraftman Hatton. Lifting off at 15:45 on 14 May, Arthur's aircraft, L-5585, was met by intense anti-aircraft and small arms fire and disappeared from view, one of seven aircraft lost by 105 Squadron during the raid. Arthur's name is recorded on the left-hand gate of the Ammanford memorial gates in Iscennen Road. 63 Battles had taken off to bomb the Meuse bridges that day. 40 failed to return, an appalling attrition rate.

Rapid evacuation from France became the imperative, with the order quickly issued to make for the channel ports. Operation Dynamo, the evacuation of over 338,000 Allied servicemen from Dunkirk, is, of course, very well known, but less so are Operation Cycle (from Le Havre) and Operation Aerial (from ports further south in western France), in which close to 200,000 soldiers and civilians left France in the days and weeks after Dunkirk had finished. Two of these were Glyn James of the RASC and Kemys Morgan of 105 Squadron.

"Were you on the train to Cherbourg?" A J C 'Bing' Eagles, pilot of 105 Squadron's Battle P-2248 – who had survived the decimating Meuse raid on 14 May in which Arthur Morgan had been killed – asked Kemys in 1987.

> No. The train was full. We were told that Cherbourg had been cut off and so we headed down to Saint-Malo. It was just the three of us: 'Tug' Wilson, Spiller and me. Spiller had only just joined us on the squadron.

Kemys' parents received a telegram saying that he was 'missing'. The three survivors of 105 Squadron left Saint-Malo by boat on 17 or 18 June, the soles of their RAF boots completely worn through. They got out in the nick of time, for Saint-Malo fell to the Germans just a few days later.

A little further north, with nothing more that could be done at Berry-au-Bac, Glyn James and his unit continued toward Dunkirk.

> When we neared Dunkirk, it was a sheer impossibility. We could see the beach was absolutely packed. They were just a jumble of everything. The roads were blocked. And I said, "Well, we can't do this. We'll try and make our way down towards the other side of France," and we went right across country and we ended up then in a little place called Saint-Nazaire.

Pauline Penrose remembered:

> My father didn't get out until after Dunkirk and we thought
> we had lost him. It turned out that they couldn't get to the
> beaches, so they were going south all the way and travelling
> at night and hiding during the day in orchards right through
> France. He managed to get back, but was in rags. It took him
> some while – we don't know how long it took him to get back.

The tragedy of the *Lancastria*

Glyn James found himself in Saint-Nazaire, on the west coast
of France, where on 17 June 1940 he witnessed the worst
disaster in British naval history. The Cunard ocean liner,
RMS *Lancastria*, now a troop ship and redesignated HMT
Lancastria, was laden with Army and Air Force personnel
trying to evacuate. It is estimated that there were anywhere
between 4,000 and 9,000 people on board, crammed into the
cargo holds and every other free space, when Junkers Ju 88
bombers came in to attack.

> We were trying to get on it. It was blown up when we were
> there. You know, we were cowering against the back walls.
> And, of course, that's when the whole thing blew up, you see?
> Horrific. There was nothing we could do about it. There were
> about five of the bombers there – bombing and strafing. One
> bomb went down the funnel and blew the thing apart.

The huge ship sank in about 15 minutes.

> That was one of the worst disasters in the whole war. There
> were well over 6,000 people that got killed and it was so bad
> Churchill said that we don't want to tell anybody about it,
> because it'll have a detrimental effect on the morale of the
> people.

The final death toll is still unknown. A memorial at the seafront at the town today commemorates 'more than 4,000' victims; others, like Glyn, believed the total was nearer 6,000.

Having witnessed the horror of that summer day, Glyn and his unit headed to La Rochelle, where he was able to persuade a French fisherman to take his unit of 30 to England. By the time they arrived, Glyn was exhausted.

> Today, if anybody gave me a million pounds to say where we landed, I couldn't tell you because I'd gone over the mark. I'd had no sleep. Nothing to eat. I was absolutely whacked.

Dunkirk – and the imminent fear of invasion – had encouraged many to join up. Charlie Barnes of Prestatyn was old enough to go into full uniform.

> I joined up just after Dunkirk. I was 18. All the lads in the street had gone, so there were not many left. There were three of us who went down and joined up. Joined the Navy. My father had been in the Navy during the First World War, so I suppose that's why. I thought it was great. In fact, when the second war started, my father went in the Army. At his age! Then they found out how old he was and they, you know, they gave him his papers and finished him. That was after Dunkirk.

Interviewed in Pembroke Dock in 2020, Gordon Prime looked back to the time when, aged 16, he sought to join the Local Defence Volunteers (LDV), later and more widely known as the Home Guard:

> In May/June 1940 we heard on the radio that the Germans were advancing to Holland, Belgium, into France, and our British Expeditionary Force was stranded on the beaches at Dunkirk. Things were pretty bad after that, talking about

the Germans invading. There again, it came on the radio one evening: would all young men from the age of 17 and older men up to the age of, I think it was 55 or 65 [it was 65], volunteer to join the Local Defence Volunteers, the LDV?

My dad being an ex-soldier from the First World War, and myself, we went up to the local police station and volunteered. "How old are you?" I said: "17" – I was only 16, but he said, "OK." So from then on, we used to report to the little village just beyond Birmingham Airport as it is now, a place called Bickenhill.

In Port Talbot, apprentice painter and decorator Archie Thomas recalled:

I joined the town Home Guard at 17. My next-door neighbour and I would do sentry duty. We would be at the old Royal Horse Artillery Barracks and inside was a settee and we used to sit in there, behind the door, from four to seven in the morning and got paid three shillings for doing the guard. I always did the morning guard and would go home then, breakfast and off to work. Cartwright was the Commanding Officer of the Home Guard for Port Talbot. He was also the head of the Port Talbot Steelworks in Margam.

Gordon Prime remembered that it took time for the Home Guard to begin to look like an organised force.

We set a guard room up in the school and the church tower was the watchtower, and we did guard duty. I think it started off with about maybe fourteen of us. We used to report every night and do two on four off. Two hours on top of the church tower, with the others getting their head down in the school room. Anyway, this went on for a time. And all we had were six First World War Lee-Enfield .303 rifles between the fourteen of us, six rounds of ammunition for each rifle and a white armband with LDV on it. The locals used to say, "Look, Duck and Vanish!"

After a time, we had denim overalls, the battledress type of overalls, which we wore – we had those as a uniform, and a forage cap. Then they gave us Army boots and gaiters. We didn't have the webbing gaiters that they issued to the British Army, we had leather gaiters, black leather gaiters – why, I don't know – and a leather belt. Then later on, we got proper battledress and began to look like soldiers then.

Many young women were also looking for ways to help the war effort. Mary Bott had been born Mary Evans in Dulwich in 1924 to Welsh parents, but in the early days of the war lived with relatives near Aberdyfi. She was eager to do her bit.

They said I could either go into munitions or on the land. Well, I chose the land, you see, although I didn't know anything about farming, really. But I did know the difference between a bull and a cow: because the bull had a ring through his nose!

I landed up in Llangeitho for a couple of months because the man who was working there was in hospital, so they needed a bit of help. When the man came back, I went to Llanarth and I worked there for nearly a year, and then I moved to a place outside Aberystwyth.

I learnt to milk cows and then I had to clean out the stables and help out with the hay. I used to get up at half past five in the morning and I wouldn't finish until half past six at night. I had fun.

We had Italian prisoners of war [working on the farm]. One said to me one day, he would like to take me for a walk with him in the woods. And I said, "No, you will get into trouble." He said, "No trouble, I have the piece of rubber!"

3

Refuge

"My mother didn't want to put me on the train because I was so ill, but our doctor friend who was putting her daughter on the train said, 'Hilda, if you don't put her on the train, she will never go.' How right she was, as Nicholas Winton's next train had the children on board, but it was the day war was declared so it never left."

RENATE COLLINS, BEM

WHILE THE TEENAGERS of Wales sought to join up, young people all over Europe had already become victims of war. The British government had changed some immigration rules to allow for child refugees from the Nazis and between December 1938 and September 1939, approximately 10,000 unaccompanied child refugees arrived in the country, on what later became known as the *Kindertransport* ('children's transport'). These were established by Jewish organisations such as the Central British Fund for German Jewry and Youth Aliyah, and also non-Jewish groups such as the Society of Friends (Quakers). Some of the most famous rescues were spearheaded by Nicholas Winton, a British banker who saved 669 children by arranging transports from Prague.

Renate Collins BEM (born Renate Kress) looked back to her early years as a 5-year-old girl living with her parents, Otto and Hilda Kress, in what was then Czechoslovakia. In March 1939, the Germans marched into Prague.

I went from my apartment to the nearby nursery school. In the March, the German soldiers entered Prague and took over the kitchens in the school down the road to my great aunt's, where I would stay until my mother picked me up, as she was a Theatre Sister in Prague Hospital.

The German soldiers were very kind to us – they gave us sweets. I suspect it all brought back memories of their children that they had left behind in Germany. I was told that they were OK, but never to have anything to do with the ones with black leather coats and black hats [Gestapo].

My great aunt [Selma] was a sculptress. So I spent many hours watching her working. She studied in Paris, France, under Rodin. She sculptured famous people which were then exhibited in Prague Museum. Unfortunately, the Germans had removed and buried them. We couldn't find out where they were buried but having been underground, they probably would have been smashed.

What did she remember of the Kindertransport journey?

I left Prague on 30 June 1939, on Nicholas Winton's train, which turned out to be his last train. I was put on the train by my mother, as only one parent was allowed to be on the platform.

I had chickenpox and a temperature of 104 and was carried onto the train. My mother didn't want to put me on the train because I was so ill, but our doctor friend who was putting her daughter on the train said, "Hilda, if you don't put her on the train, she will never go." How right she was, as Nicholas Winton's next train had the children on board, but it was the day war was declared so it never left.

I don't remember the journey as I was lying down. I was carried from the Prague train to the ferry at the Hook of Holland. I remember being seasick and at Harwich being taken to the train for Liverpool Street station.

All children under 7 years old had to have a home to go to. My foster family had received letters from my mother and photographs had been exchanged. So, at Liverpool Street station I was given to this tall gentleman. He had a black suit, coat and black hat and a 'dog collar', as he was a Baptist minister, and off we went to Wales.

The government allowed 10,000 refugees to come to the UK. Everyone that came in had to be sponsored £50 [worth over £4,000 today] each for the visas for our entry. We never found out who paid my £50 on the register which was kept by Nicholas Winton, which is now at the Yad Vashem Museum in Jerusalem. Opposite my name is 'Guaranteed', and then the address where I was going. Above my name were 13 other children who had been sponsored by a Lord and Lady, who had obviously sponsored £650, but they didn't house any [children] so that was their contribution.

I've got letters my mother wrote to Wales and one was dictated by me saying I hoped there was no spinach in England but if there was plenty of ice cream, I could be a good girl. As there was not much ice cream during the war, I don't know if I was a good girl or not!

I went to school in Porth in September '39 and my foster father was very intent on me learning English properly. When I went to the senior school, I was either top or second in English grammar. He insisted I did a spelling challenge every night. On going to the senior school, I was put into the German class, where I came bottom of the class, although I had been German-speaking [Renate's father was originally from Germany]. Many years later, my friend of 83 years (who had seen me asleep the morning after I arrived) and I were talking about my lapse of memory on relearning my initial language and we both came to the conclusion that it was psychological and that my brain didn't want to re-engage with the past. I suppose that was understandable. I did better in Latin, French and Welsh classes.

At the end of the war, I'd been in Wales longer than I'd been in Prague and my time was occupied with learning the language and education. I had spoken Czech and German so to learn a new language at 6 years old was a big thing with no interpreters!

Vera Buchthal was also 5 years old when she arrived in Britain as a Jewish refugee. Born in Dortmund, Germany, she left on a Kindertransport from Vienna after her mother decided to send her and her 9-year-old sister, also named Renate, to safety. Now known as Stephanie Shirley, and having been made a Dame and a Companion of Honour for services to business and philanthropy, she found refuge in England but developed many connections to Wales.

> When I got to Oswestry, the co-ed school apparently announced two little refugee girls were arriving and they would be very disturbed, and everyone was to be very nice to us. Certainly, that happened. We were not made to feel unwelcome at all. I needed those six years of peace in Oswestry to begin to put down roots. I was very conscious that Oswestry is politically English but geographically Wales. On market day, the farmers came down from the hills with their cattle and the whole town spoke Welsh, which I do not. It was a very warm community.
>
> The other link that got us to Wales was my father's story. In 1940 he was interned as an adult German to New South Wales, Australia, and then got the opportunity to come out of his internment camp and join the Pioneer Corps in England. First he was in Bicester and then he was put in charge of what became the Mid Wales Psychiatric Hospital at Talgarth. So, for several years we would occasionally see him at Talgarth. I can remember picking bilberries on the Brecon Beacons and really feeling the mountain environment that I was accustomed to in Austria.

There are lots of things that make Wales very dear to me. I can remember my tears of joy when I heard people singing spontaneously on the trains – maybe I was going to Talgarth – which would happen very much in continental Europe. And I sang in my school choir at the Eisteddfod in Llangollen one year. I had the feeling it was a quiet and musical country that valued education, and I think that resonated with me, even as a child.

Renate Collins remembered:

After the war finished, I didn't find out anything about my family until the end of 1946, beginning of 1947, because I had no one left in Prague. My second cousin, Lisl, was a dress designer during the war for Marks and Spencer and was able to go to Prague on a trade visa. She was my mother's age and so knew more of the family. She found that 64 members of the family had died.

I only knew the five nearest to me, who are my father, mother, grandmother, my mother's brother Felix (whom I don't remember being there often, as he was in the Czech Army), and my great aunt Selma (the sculptress), with whom I spent a lot of time. She died in Łódź; my father and Felix died in Auschwitz.

After finding out this out, I was able to become a British subject and was then adopted by Sidney and Arianwen Coplestone. The last communication from my family was for my birthday in 1942, dated 10 June, and signed 'Mama, Grandmamma, Felix', which came via the Red Cross.

It said on my mother and grandmother's death certificates that they died at Treblinka... But three years ago, while my youngest son Peter was in Israel, he went to the Yad Vashem Museum and looked up the records. I found out they were being taken by train from Terezin, which was a 'holding camp', to Treblinka. On the way, the train broke down and, instead of waiting for the train to be repaired, they were shot and then taken to Treblinka to be buried. 988,000 Jews were buried there. It took me 80 years to find this out.

A few years ago, there was a TV programme about Treblinka. In 1944, Hitler decided to expose the graves and burn them. A lady came on and she said she remembered the village being told to keep their windows and doors closed. Not to go out. She said, "I can still smell it." No grass grew for 20 years afterwards. When my two sons went to Auschwitz, they asked whether there was anything at Treblinka in memory and were told "No", but [since then] there have been stones put up. That was interesting for me to find out.

In the early 1990s we had some school reunions. I didn't remember any of the boys from my classes; it was a mixed school, and we girls were glad to go to our own playground. A former pupil was at my table during one reunion, and he said, "Do you remember saving me from having a beating?" I said no. He said a boy was on top of him, kicking him and beating him. I came up, didn't say a word, got hold of the boy's collar, and pulled him off, and then walked away. Obviously, I didn't want anybody to be ill-treated.

4

Bombers Over Wales

"The next moment there is this almighty flash, purple
and blue, and I can remember like today: the blast
punched me in the chest and I went flying backwards,
and I don't remember any more after that."

TED OWENS

Inferno at Pembroke Dock

This was to be the first major war in which civilian populations
in Wales would be the target of heavy bombing raids.

Pembroke Dock became an early priority target for the
Luftwaffe because it was a military town used by the Navy,
Army and RAF. It was also the location of large oil storage
tanks, and these were photographed by a lone German spy
plane in the summer of 1940. The Germans then sent over
the bombers. It was a sunny August afternoon in 1940, but
a single bomb was about to start one of the fiercest fires of
the war.

John Brock, who later devoted his life to running the
Carew Cheriton Control Tower as a museum, recalled:

Our first sound was the explosion and then, all of a sudden,
the pall of smoke, the huge plume of black smoke that went
up into the sky, and eventually it had the effect that it made
it look almost like evening coming in. When the pall got in
front of the sun, it seemed to dim the whole area.

One of the tanks had taken a direct hit and burst into flames. Over the next three weeks, more than 600 men would fight the blaze. Among them was rookie auxiliary fireman Wyndham Scourfield of Narberth.

> I joined the fire service in June 1940. My birthday was 12 August, and the tanker fire was on the 19th – my first job!
>
> Everything was alright until you got a matter of about half a mile or so from the Dock, and then you could see this terrific amount of smoke and the nearer you got, the denser it got, until in the end – well, you could only go at walking pace with the vehicles.

Mounds of earth – called bunds – had been built around the oil tanks. The firemen had to stand on them to fight the fire.

> Chaps had sheets of old zinc, an old door or something like that, with a hole knocked into the sheet. The branch, or the hose, was put through that hole and you had this sheet of zinc protecting you. It was absolute chaos.

Full-time firefighters from as far away as Birmingham and Cardiff came to fight the blaze.

> They did some marvellous work. One chap [went] to the top of the tank and put a plug of wood in a hole that was there and this type of thing, and it was about that time that these poor boys were lost in the fire.

Five men from Cardiff were killed instantly when they were engulfed in flames. They were Frederick George Davies (31), Ivor John Kilby (29), Clifford Mills (31), Trevor Charles Morgan (31) and John Frederick Thomas (30).

Ted Owens, messenger boy with the Pembroke Dock fire service, remembered:

One of the tanks exploded with the heat from the other tanks. They were dowsing it with water and they had foam being pumped into the top of the tanks, but they still failed to keep it cool enough and the tank exploded, and five firemen were caught in the flames when it busted.

Ted was only 16 years old.

Of course, being young and dull, I think I knew of every bomb dropped in Pembrokeshire and I would go and have look, being right nosey. One night in particular, they were dropping the bombs and I was standing outside of the door [of the fire station] as usual, and most of the firemen were inside. I spotted this big parachute coming down and I said, "Oh look, there's a parachute coming down."

The next moment there is this almighty flash, purple and blue, and I can remember like today: the blast punched me in the chest and I went flying backwards, and I don't remember any more after that. Apparently, the men said I went past them like a rocket into the fire station behind the fire engine and finished up in a corner, and of course all the stuff that was on the shelves had all come down on top of me – pots of paint and all that, though none of them opened up. I don't remember any more about it until I woke up in the control room on one of the camp beds and one of the telephone girls washing my mouth out and my face, because there was so much dust everywhere that I was nearly blinded with it. I got up none the worse and once I was on my feet, I was okay.

Duncan Hilling, who was born and bred in Saundersfoot, was 14 at the time.

I remember going out with my father into our fields and we could see the flames and heard the bombs dropping on Pembroke Dock, and of course they set fire to the oil depots there, which burned for some weeks. It was a huge problem in our area because there were masses of black smoke and for a few weeks no one could hang clothes out, because they would be covered with black smoke and oil from Pembroke Dock. It was a nasty experience.

For 18 days the fire blazed at Pembroke Dock. Almost 100,000 tons of oil was destroyed. The site is now a golf course, but a memorial plaque ensures that the firemen's bravery and sacrifice continue to be remembered.

The bombers come for Cardiff and Swansea

Towards the end of 1940 and into the first months of 1941, the Luftwaffe's attacks spread further afield. Bristol, Manchester, Liverpool and Birmingham were amongst the English cities and towns badly hit, and in Wales, Cardiff and Swansea took the brunt.

On 2 January 1941, 100 German bombers attacked Cardiff, with Riverside and Grangetown taking real poundings from the high explosive bombs, parachute mines and incendiaries. It was the largest single bombing raid of the war in Wales. The target was the docks at Cardiff, but residential areas were badly damaged too.

Syd Daw, aged 15, had left his home in Hillsnook Road in Ely to go to the nearby Avenue Cinema with his family.

When they thought there was an air-raid coming, you'd be warned, "There's an air-raid going on" – you'd hear the sirens going, anyway. And you could leave the cinema if you wanted to, but they'd carry on showing the film. So my mother and sister wanted to go home. I said, "Oh, let's see the film first" – you know, old clever sticks! And so we did. We saw the film. As we came out onto the steps, you can look across Cardiff and Cardiff was ablaze. All these incendiary bombs had been dropped. You would think the whole city of Cardiff was alight. Very sad and frightening. And, of course, there's guns going up and down the main road, firing at planes and so on. So that was a nasty one.

Turning for home, one bomber dropped a parachute mine which badly damaged Llandaff Cathedral. The roof crashed in and destroyed much of the interior. But because the cathedral is in a dip, many of the houses on the Green, a short distance away, escaped serious damage.

Margaret Samuel was one of those who could have been killed had the mine blown on a slightly different course. Speaking in 2011, Margaret stated:

It's only recently I've realised that I was near death at that time, because if it had been just up on the top by the cross and by the Green – 'cos we're, what, 50 metres or whatever it is from the Green – I wouldn't be here today.

Although she was only 7 at the time, that night of horror was imprinted on her memory.

It was such a wonderful night. It was a full moon, what they called a 'hunter's moon'. That night the hunters were the Luftwaffe.

Her family was forced from their shelter by a fireman banging on the front door.

And he shouted, "Get out! The house is on fire, you've been hit by a bomb, get out!" And I ran out past him into the street, screaming. I didn't go back to my mother and my brother: it was self-preservation!

The flares were all around. They were dropping flares, lighting everything up. And also incendiary bombs. And we were trying to avoid being hit by any of these things.

As I was running with all this, I was screaming my head off. I thought, 'This is what hell must be like' – you know, with all these flames, I mean. It was terrifying.

The death toll across Cardiff that night was 165, with 427 injured. The greatest single death toll was in Grangetown, where many had taken shelter in the basement of Hollyman's Bakery.

Ken Lloyd had been to a children's party and was walking home when the sirens sounded.

I got as far as Hollyman's and he was calling everybody into the shelter – for safety, of course. And I said, "No, I won't come in, I haven't got far to go. I'll carry on and go home."

More than 30 people crowded into the makeshift shelter, listening as the bombs began to fall. One went straight through the building and exploded in the basement, killing them all. The next morning, Ken walked through the street and saw only rubble where the bakery had stood.

In the industrial port of Swansea, Enid Lloyd (later Enid Lewis), daughter of a Welsh suffragette, and about to be called up to become an aircraft plotter in the ATS (Auxiliary Territorial Service), made a succinct note in her diary on 17 February 1941:

Swansea was bombed. Megan, Sammy, Derrick and I were caught in the Air Raid, so we sheltered in the London Inn and had a game of darts.

In Port Talbot, Archie Thomas recalls having a grandstand seat for the Luftwaffe's bombing of Swansea.

We could see the bombers going over to Swansea. My brother and I heard the air raid sirens going off, planes overhead. We dashed upstairs, looking out of the window, and all of sudden 'whooooeee'. It was a bomb. It had dropped in Leslie Street [in Port Talbot]. There were two or three killed. We jumped down the bloody stairs!

Soon after, Swansea became the only major Welsh town to suffer raids across three consecutive nights: 19, 20 and 21 February 1941.

On duty was Elaine Kidwell, a 17-year-old who had started as a messenger, receiving lessons in underground warfare. Speaking in 2011, she remembered:

We had to know, if anything went wrong and the Germans invaded, how to defend ourselves. So they had us jump out of first-floor windows on to mock-ups of tanks and lift the lid up – I still laugh at this – light our bombs, what we call today some cocktails or something ['Molotov Cocktails'], and put it in and put the lid down and get off. And I turned to the chap who was telling us and said, "What would the Germans be doing when we do this?", and he said, "Well, we don't know, but we're hoping it will surprise them!" So we'd have all been dead, you know!

As the Luftwaffe raids on Swansea and its surrounding areas became increasingly withering, there was a call in Llanelli for firefighters and Mary Walker (now Mary Griffiths) volunteered. After training, she was issued with a card dated 13.10.41, which said: 'Mary Walker is appointed one of the Town Centre Fire Fighters.' Mary was just 17.

By the night of the start of the Blitz, Elaine Kidwell was an air raid warden – despite being underage.

I was a messenger and along came the head of the ARP and he said, "How old are you now, exactly?" I said, "I'm 17 and three months," and he said, "Oh, you're in your 18th year, then. Now, it says here that you have to be 18 to be an air raid warden, but we'll bend the rules – you're in!" So that's how I was a warden.

It is hard to imagine now how it must have felt when the sirens sounded and the city waited for the Luftwaffe bombers. Elaine said:

They were across Devon and across the Bristol Channel in minutes. We could hear them coming across the bay.

Fred and Kate Garland had been make-up artists for stars appearing at Swansea's Palace Theatre in the 1920s and owned five hairdresser's shops in the town. Fred was also an air raid warden during the three nights of the Swansea Blitz. Watching with grave concern from the railings opposite 34 Crescent Road, Llandeilo were Fred and Kate's daughters Phyllis Evans and Dot Spurway, who had been evacuated there with their respective children, Joan and Michael, and Pam and Peter. The sky beyond the ornate iron railings opposite the house blazed red as the Luftwaffe bombs cascaded down upon Swansea, with the distant yet still very audible explosions echoing across the rolling hills beyond Llandeilo. Fred and Kate survived but over the three nights of the Swansea Blitz, three of their salons were destroyed.

From his home in Llandybie, 8-year-old Don Davies watched the bombing of Swansea in awe.

We could see from our home the red glow of the fires high above the oil works in Llandarcy, which was well alight. We heard the bombings on Swansea itself and the sounds of the Heinkel bombers, which had a humming noise – their throbbing 'ummmm ummmm' sounded as if they were diesel engines, although I am not sure today whether they were or not. Swansea was really well alight and, as far as we were concerned on King's Road, we could have very well been able to read a newspaper in the glow of fires given from the oil works in Llandarcy. After the bombings, we went down during the day into Swansea and saw all the rubble strewn everywhere with bulldozers clearing this, and to us at our age it was an exciting outing really. We weren't old enough, really, to realise fully what was going on.

Llansamlet-born Richard Pelzer, a 16-year-old stonemason, had to venture into the town on the second day of the raids. Interviewed a few weeks before his 100th birthday in 2024, he remembered that the raid started as he made his way home.

A policeman shouted, "Get down! Get down!" And there was a lot of debris flying, and with that, *bomp!*, the barbershop window I was sheltering by came out. And when it came down, a couple of pieces fell on me and of course I got cut and everything.

I went to an emergency first-aid place. They did me up a bit and then I made my way home. And, of course, I had a telling off when I got home.

But talk about Blackpool Illuminations! With the incendiary bombs going off, it was like nobody's business. The town was really floodlit.

I didn't go to town for a long while after that, because the memory was there. There were big lumps taken out of a wall in Orchard Street and they are still there.

Caught up in the middle of the raids, over three nights Elaine Kidwell was to see the best and worst of humanity. Death from the air, courage on the ground. She narrowly escaped being killed when a parachute mine exploded above her head.

Everybody was blown, and I was blown right across the road, crashed into a wall, and I didn't have any breath in me.

Anyway, I was coming around, and I went into my pocket – and I wish I hadn't, because I've had my leg pulled about it ever since – I took my lipstick out and I put it on. And one of the wardens said, "That's your armour, isn't it?" I said, "Yes. As long as I've got my lipstick on, I can face anything!"

Swansea's historic town centre, including the Ben Evans department store, a jewel in its crown, was being destroyed.

[The city] burned from Castle Street right along to where the YMCA is now. We went up now to do what we could at the top of Wind Street, and some people started to come up Caer Street at the side and we had to scream at them to go back because the Ben Evans [store] was coming over.

St Mary's [Church] was burning, flames were coming up, even up the great tower, and the bells were crashing down. And I was very young then… I was 17 then, and that's like a 12-year-old now. I said to Mr Scott, our head warden, "They are definitely going to lose the war." He said, "How's that, *bach*?" I said, "They've burned God's house down, and he's not going to have that" – and you know what you are when you're full of it. And he went, "Yes, alright."

The whole town was burning. I thought the world was on fire. It was terrible to see your lovely town burning. They had meant to wreck the town and they did.

Elaine may have felt like a young 17-year-old, but she grew up quickly over those nights of horror.

I could see Mr Scott kneeling on the ground beside a body. So I ran up, and he said, "Take your lanyard off" – my precious Guide lanyard. So I took it off. He said, "Put it on his leg." Now, it was black: the only light we had were the gun flashes. "Where?" I said. "On the knee." "Well, where's the rest of his leg?" "It's over there somewhere."

Somebody saw what was happening, and rushed to the
phone, and got us what we called an ambulance – it was
a beat-up old van with a bit of linoleum down the back,
because ambulances were all over the place. So they carried
him in and the medics said to us, "You've done a good job.
He's lost his leg, but he's going to live."

Now, that was a good moment.

Later, Elaine heard that her cousins' home had been hit and
the bodies had been moved to a church.

There were two coffins there for Mummy and Daddy, and one
little square coffin, white, like that, with two babies in. The
little baby of… she was about three months old, was lying
on her back, and the little boy, her brother, he was about 18
months, they put him facing her with his arm on her. That
finished me. I'll never forget that little white coffin.

On the night of 21 February 1941, Swansea suffered its third
night in a row of heavy bombing. It was the first city outside
London to suffer that fate.

They were coming in waves, one after another. [On] the
other raids, I noticed that there weren't so many planes, and
between times there would be a lull, but they were coming
over so fast, I don't know how the firemen came through it. It
must have been dreadful for them.

In one bomb-torn street, Elaine crawled into a cellar to check
on a family sheltering from the raid.

I saw them all: they were all sleeping, not a mark on them.
'Lovely,' I thought. The others pulled me up and I said,
"They're all asleep, they're alright." "Alright," they said. And
the head warden and deputy head warden, my father, said to

me, "Go back to the post now and see if there's any messages for us, and as you're there, put the kettle on and the mugs out and take your time."

A short while later, Elaine returned to the scene.

They were just bringing [the family] out: they were all dead. The blast had killed them. And I couldn't believe it. The expression on their faces was quite normal, not frightened. The blast killed them and killed them instantly: it took all the breath out of their body. As my dad said, they didn't know anything.

Elaine Kidwell's concluding thoughts on the horror of the Blitz:

It was very frightening, and the rest of your life you say with all humility, "Thank you, God, for getting me through."
I think everybody felt like that, because it was horrific.

5

Training for War

"My mother cried and my father said,
'Well, that'll make a man out of him.'"
DENNIS TIDSWELL

BY 3 SEPTEMBER 1939, the three branches of the British Armed Services were by varying degrees a little more attuned to the threat posed by Herr Hitler than Chamberlain had been less than 12 months earlier in Munich.

Royal Air Force and Women's Auxiliary Air Force

Of the services, the Royal Air Force had received the firmest backing from the Cabinet in Westminster and had implemented a series of expansion schemes between 1934 and 1938. It had also laid the ground for the eventual Empire Air Training Plan, which was to provide the training of aircrew in several countries free from Luftwaffe attack and with sunnier climates.

With the imminent Fall of France in May 1940, this plan kicked into reality, with the first cadets being sent out to Southern Rhodesia (now Zimbabwe), followed in turn by Canada (where most were trained), South Africa, and then covertly to the USA, prior to its entry to war following the Japanese attack on Pearl Harbor on 7 December 1941. In fact, many Fleet Air Arm pilots were also trained in Michigan and Pensacola. Over the duration of the war, 220,000 RAF and FAA aircrew were trained for service overseas, including many from Wales.

Recruitment of RAF personnel was never going to be a problem as eager, if rather naïve, young men and women clamoured to join, serving in many differing capacities and theatres of war.

In the early summer of 1940, Dennis Tidswell was an Aircraftman Second Class, "at the bottom of the pecking order". He recalled:

After about four or five days [in tents at RAF Uxbridge], we were then put into a billet, as it was called. It was like a Nissen-hut with a cast-iron pipe stove.

There was a Corporal's room at the end, and the Corporal was invariably a regular airman and a charming sort of chap, because he would wake you up in the morning – very politely… "Come on, you sods – wakey, wakey; get your hands off your cocks and get moving, and stand by your beds, it's eight o' clock."

We were all lined up for inoculations – anti-tetanus and typhoid… so, there stood two men in white coats. I presumed one was a doctor, and there's a high table, three kidney-shaped, white-enamelled dishes with a blue rim around the top, filled with methylated spirits. And there were two rather large needles. The actual needle of which was not like any refined one that there is nowadays. It was nearly like a very fine nail really. Anyway, there were hundreds of blokes all lined up to see two people. You came along, got it jabbed into your arm, and then that particular needle was thrown into the dish of meths where the other man rinsed it out, and refilled it in sequence. So those two needles really injected hundreds of men.

And then one day we were all marched up to this large room and all seated down in front of a screen, cinema fashion, and we were shown a film about venereal disease. Now, looking at it, ages 18 to 25-ish, the likes of me, who'd never had any sexual education at all – either school, college or anywhere. This film showed the graphic detail, the horrors of gonorrhoea. And in the end, it showed us a chappie having rather like a violent epileptic fit, who was in the advanced stages of syphilitic infection, but at least it taught most of us something of which we had precious little knowledge.

Around the same time as Dennis, Trevor Jones from Letterston, Pembrokeshire had enlisted in the RAF. Trevor later followed a protracted route to operational flying.

> I went for initial training to Bridlington in East Yorkshire, to do my square-bashing there. From there I went to White Waltham near Maidenhead, to the De Havilland Flying School, as a member of the RAF Regiment doing just guard duties and general 'muck about'.
>
> I was there for probably about a year, then 're-mustered', I think the word was, and sent to RAF Cranwell, where I did a wireless and radio operator course. I was then a radio operator at a DF [Direction Finding] station in Newcastle upon Tyne. There were Spitfire squadrons stationed around there, and I was stuck in a ploughed field with this DF truck, where I would be giving bearings to whichever aircraft was in trouble and wanted a bearing to come home.
>
> I got rather fed up with this sort of life, and on the Daily Orders, the RAF said they wanted air gunners because they were short. So I put my name down, and that started me on a flying career.

The Women's Auxiliary Air Force was a big pull for many women. Although her brother was serving in the Royal Navy, Adelaide Jarman had been determined to join the WAAFs. In 2021, sitting alongside her husband of 76 years, John (of whom we will learn more later), in their home at Tan-y-groes, near Aberporth, Adelaide recalled her time in basic training at RAF Morecambe Bay.

> We seemed to do a lot of marching and saluting there, but for us there were no seaside pleasures!

She had hoped to become an aircraft plotter but, being a little colour-blind, had failed her eye test and was asked if she would be prepared to train as a flight mechanic, to which she readily agreed.

After training at No. 6 School of Technical Training at RAF Hednesford in Staffordshire, where Royal Air Force and Fleet Air Arm mechanics together received technical training on a variety of airframes and engines, Adelaide was posted to RAF Little Rissington in the Cotswolds. This was the home of No. 6 Service Flying Training School and also No. 8 Maintenance Unit. Suddenly, Adelaide's job at this airfield was not to be trained but to train others, by maintaining aircraft in which the bomber crews of the future were being prepared for war.

> I worked throughout on Airspeed Oxfords. All the girls [flight mechanics] worked exceedingly well together – it took two people to do a daily inspection of an Oxford. We had to be agile – working at height on the back of a propellor, walking along the top of the fuselage, taking a petrol hose off the bowser and crawling, dragging the hose onto the aircraft, and then putting the nozzle into place. The engine mechanic would read the petrol gauge, though intuitively she would know how much was being put in.
>
> I was the airframe mechanic and often the crew of the Oxford I was working on would come milling around when I was checking the ailerons, flaps, etc. They'd ask, "So, when are you going to sign up [form 700], so we can take off?"

These were aircrew keen to get in their flying hours, in order to be posted to an operational squadron somewhere. We were very keen to do everything right, because we knew the men who were going to be flying in these aircraft. Myself and another girl sat in the cockpit and ran the engines. My friends Freda and Anne became very worried if an engine didn't make the right noise. In fact, Anne would suddenly wake up in the middle of the night and shout out that an engine was going to blow a gasket, and we would shout at her to go back to sleep!

We worked very hard. We had a real bond with these aircraft and occasionally would get to fly with a crew, but you could only fly when Sergeant Kemahan gave permission – and only when he allowed us to go up with experienced pilots! You also needed to find a crew member willing to let you borrow their parachute.

George Duffee of Aberaeron wanted to be a fighter pilot and even lied about his age to join the RAF. Interviewed during a visit to an Evasion Lines Memorial Society event at Eden Camp in York, he stated:

I trained in America. Got my wings at age 18, because I'd falsified my age by one year to get into the conflict. And the air force, the Royal Air Force, still think I was 19 when I got my wings, but I was actually 18 – so I could fly an aeroplane, but I didn't know how to drive a car!

We all wanted to be fighter pilots, you see, but we came back [from America] and all the losses were in Bomber Command, and so we were automatically in Bomber Command through the Wellington [bombers] OTU – Operational Training Unit – which was up at Lossiemouth. And then through what they called the 'heavy conversion unit'. It's rather interesting how you select crews, because you think – you know, these are the chaps who are going to risk their lives with you, and you're going to rely on them and you'll rely on each other, but it is all done rather cordially. You were just all put in a huge hangar and told, "Right, get on with it," by the CO [Commanding Officer]. And it worked out beautifully. There were very few cases where people didn't like their navigator or the bomb-aimer or whatever.

The pilot is always the captain. It could be an NCO [Non-Commissioned Officer] pilot, and he could have a navigator who is an officer, but the captain of the aircraft was always in charge.

Fred Seal from Barry was in the RAF too. A 16-year-old apprentice carpenter when the war started, Fred had joined the Air Training Corps before finally getting the call to go to Lord's Cricket Ground, which had become the Air Crew Reception Centre.

It was where all pilots, navigators and bomb-aimers went. After Lord's, I went down to Babbacombe to No. 1 ITW [Initial Training Wing]. I was told I was going to be a bomb-aimer.

I went on a boat to South Africa and as we went into Durban harbour, a lady was singing from the end of the docks. Her name was Perla Gibson. She was an operatic singer. She wore a white dress, a red hat and she had a marvellous voice. What amazed me was, she even sang to the troops when she learnt that her son had been killed.

Fred's bomb-aimer training took place at Port Elizabeth (now known as Gqeberha).

The aircraft we flew in was the good old Avro Anson and the Airspeed Oxford, better known as an Ox Box. In the daytime you dropped a smoke bomb; at night you dropped a flash bomb.

Fred was soon on the move again: this time to RAF Ismailia in Egypt, where he was trained to crew a long-range Consolidated Liberator bomber.

> I have one horrible memory of crawling down into the bomb section where the bomb bay was, and the person who'd been there before me had been sick all over it and they couldn't clean it up in time, but we still had to fly. The training Sergeant was shouting at me, "Get down there!"

On a bombing run, the pilot listened to the bomb-aimer's every word as he lay in the belly of the aircraft, watching as they approached the target.

At home, the perilous nature and inherent dangers involved in flying training were consistently downplayed to the public by the authorities. Sadly, the hills and mountains of Wales became littered with the wrecks of aircraft and young crews lost, but there were also losses on the ground.

On Sunday, 9 April 1944, 25-year-old WAAF Dorothy Evans was asleep in her barracks alongside 15 others at RAF Fairwood Common, Swansea, when a four-engine Halifax bomber on a training flight crashed into the barracks, killing Dorothy and injuring the others. Dorothy's name is included on the war memorial plaque in Tal-y-bont Memorial Hall, Ceredigion and her relatives, some of whom still live in the Tal-y-bont area, still think of her 80 years later.

From her home in Aberporth, Jean McKay looked back to her training as a WAAF – but also to the period before that, when she worked inside the corridors of power in Whitehall during the Blitz.

> If anything had been bombed the night before, they would send it through on a teleprompter and we'd have to take it down to Mr Churchill in the War Rooms. And if anything needed repairing, he'd arrange for it to be repaired. He was

very nice. He just said "Good morning" when I handed him the information, that was all, but I was only 17 at the time.

But from personally handing messages on the previous night's bombing to the Prime Minister, young Jean quickly became ambitious for more adventure.

In those days, you had get permission from your father if you were under 21 years old. Eventually I did wear my father down, but it was rather against his wishes that I joined the Women's Auxiliary Air Force in February 1941. At the initial interview we were asked which trade we would prefer. I was given the choice between Meteorology and Catering. As I didn't fancy cooking, I plumped for Meteorology, although I had not the foggiest idea at all what it was!

After basic training, Jean was posted back to London to do a six-week course in Meteorology.

We learned to plot maps and read barometers and use the teleprinter – forerunner of today's sophisticated computers and scanners, but a lot noisier! After passing our final exams, we got our first proper posting. Mine was to Prestwick in Scotland, where I met my husband. Prestwick was an Air Transport Auxiliary [ATA] station which flew planes all over the country. All the pilots were volunteers who had either passed the age for call-up or were of foreign nationality and came from all over the world: Spanish, Canadian, Indian, American, British and many more.

There were many women pilots. They wore a navy-blue uniform and were a law unto themselves, but it was a very dangerous job for once they had taken off, they had no radio contact for security reasons. Quite a few were lost in bad weather, especially over the mountains. The station was run by Admiral Boucher, who didn't approve of WAAF assistants, and my future husband – who was in charge of the office in Prestwick – was told to keep a close eye on us!

Jean and H H McKay (himself later to be decorated for playing a key role in analysing the weather conditions which determined the date of the D-Day invasion of Normandy), got engaged in 1942 and married in 1943.

Royal Navy

Since 1937, British shipbuilding had been at full capacity, partly due to a desire to maintain parity of power between the Royal Navy and the sea forces of Germany and Japan. The Fleet Air Arm transferred from the RAF to the Royal Navy, though too late to ensure re-equipping with modern aircraft before the outbreak of war. Unusually, Cowbridge-born Tony Bird, who spent the early war years at school in Lampeter, joined the Royal Navy, transferred to the Fleet Air Arm for a while, and then returned to the Royal Navy for the rest of the war.

By the end of 1942, having completed convoys in the Atlantic and Mediterranean on an E-Class Destroyer, HMS *Escapade*, he was posted to HMS *King Alfred*, a Royal Navy training college in Hove, where he was promoted to Temporary Midshipman.

A Fleet Order appeared on the noticeboard asking people to volunteer as Fleet Air Arm pilots. As I was at a dead-end waiting for another ship, and nothing seemed to be happening, I volunteered and went for an interview, and I was put forward for a draft called the Admiral Tower Scheme, which meant we would be sent for training to America, to be trained by Marines.

And that's what happened – I went across to America, I think in about June of '43, and went to Grosse Ile, having landed at Halifax, Nova Scotia, in a snowstorm. I always remember we travelled to Detroit by train, and although the railway carriage had double-glazing, the snow was blowing in on us sleeping in our seats – very, very cold.

Grosse Ile was an eye-opener. American Marine pilots trained us: very, very good and efficient, mostly young people. I was taught to fly by an Ensign and also by a Lieutenant on Stearmans, a very nice and very capable aircraft, very steady – it must have been, for me to fly it! I went solo after about 12 hours, and stayed at Grosse Ile for about three months, clocking up 50–60 hours of flying time.

The American Marine pilots were very meticulous, always telling us to be aware of where we could land if your engine failed, and on one occasion, I actually had engine failure. I landed at a farm. I think it was in the middle of a maize crop, and the farmer came out in consternation because we'd ruined quite a bit of his land. When he discovered I was British, he wanted to know if I'd just flown the Atlantic, which was rather amusing!

This went on for some weeks – and then I was asked by Lieutenant Commander Jackson RN to report to his office, where he advised me that I was going to leave the course and would be returned to the UK to join the fleet somewhere, and that happened. I returned after about a couple of weeks spent in New York waiting for a ship.

In hindsight, and most likely because of his previous operational experience with the Navy (which many of the other FAA cadet pilots would not have had), it would today appear that Tony had been posted back to the UK with a view to preparing for D-Day.

Born in 1922, Neville Bowen from Ammanford had been desperate to join his brothers, who were already involved in the fight against Hitler. Due to his age, Neville's father needed to give permission for him to join the Navy. His father refused. After jobs as a miner and then in demolition, Neville was then of an age to be called up.

> I went to do my [six weeks'] training in north Wales at
> HMS *Glendower* [which became Butlin's Holiday Camp
> Pwllheli after the war, and is now the Hafan y Môr Haven
> Holiday site]. I then went to Liverpool, to HMS *Wellesley*,
> for a gunnery course and then to pick up my first ship in the
> Orkneys. This ship was the *Louis Pasteur* and it was a troop
> ship carrying RAF personnel to Canada.

After arriving in Halifax, Nova Scotia, Neville spent the next
six days travelling down to San Francisco by train to join a
merchant ship.

> When we were in gunnery training in Liverpool, one of the
> instructors had shown us an Oerlikon gun, which was an
> American gun. He told us, "Don't worry about this, you won't
> see it." But when we went on to this merchant ship in San
> Francisco and all the equipment was being brought aboard,
> the guns were already there for us to start looking at, and the
> first thing we saw was an Oerlikon. Now, we had only seen a
> glimpse of an Oerlikon in Liverpool. The magazine was a big
> cup with about 60 rounds in it and we had no idea. Anyway,
> we did manage to work it out.

Special Forces

Training for World War Two's 'Special Forces', which
included the Royal Marines Commandos, Royal Navy Beach
Commandos and the Parachute Regiment, proved gruelling
and certainly not for the faint-hearted.

Fire brigade messenger boy Ted Owens had seen his
hometown of Pembroke Dock take a terrible pasting from
German bombers.

> I wanted to take a little bit of revenge – I know that's not a
> nice word, but it's true. I wanted to find a bit of action to get
> my own back. Anyway, we were called up. I put in for the

Navy and my brother put in for the Air Force. They put him in the Navy and stuck me in the Marines!

The Marines also grabbed hold of Idwal Symonds, who had been born in November 1923 on a farm in the village of Llanddeiniolen, outside Caernarfon. He looked back at how he came to join them:

> I remember volunteering on my 18th birthday, much to the annoyance of my mother. And I volunteered originally for the Fleet Air Arm. But I failed the exam for that because I didn't think in English. I was from a Welsh-speaking family.
>
> I walked out of the interview, down a long flight of stairs, and at the foot of the staircase there were two Royal Marines in their blue uniforms. And obviously they had been primed, because they said to me, "You don't look very happy, young man." And I said, "Well, I've just been turned down."
>
> "Why don't you join the Marines?" they said. I'd never thought of the Marines – I knew nothing about them – so I said, "OK." I went upstairs with them, filled in some forms, and then went home.

Archie Thomas, from Port Talbot, remembered:

> I volunteered for the Royal Navy on 2 July 1942… and was transferred to Hayling Island on the Landing Craft and was there a fortnight when my name came out: "Thomas", "Aye?" There were six of us transferred up to Scotland, to Achnacarry, and that was hell! Some failed and went back to the Navy.

Achnacarry Castle in the Scottish Highlands was where a special camp had been created to train the new Commando fighting force. Ted Owens said:

They reckon all Commandos are volunteers, but that's a load of rubbish! I wasn't a volunteer. They sent me to Achnacarry in Scotland, which was the hardest training school in the world, so I've been told.

When we got there, we got out of the train, but we didn't get out on the platform: they stopped the train on the opposite platform, so you had to get out, jump down on the railway lines and up onto the platform on the other side. Then we had exactly one hour to get to the camp. They told us if we didn't get to the camp in that time, we'd be put back on the train and sent back to our units. That was the start of it! And from there on, I don't think we ever stopped running or fast walking.

When we got to the camp, as we got into the camp entrance, they had graves either side and they were so authentic and they stuck in your brain. One said, 'This man forgot to throw his grenade'; another: 'This man was killed by his pal because he didn't check his rifle.' Things like that. And that stuck in your mind.

And then, of course, all our training was very, very strict. Everything you did, you had to do at the double. You know, if you only went to the toilet, you had to do that at the double. If you went to the canteen, you know, you had to double it; if you went to the wash house you had to double it. There was no such thing as marching. It was all part of your training to get you really super-fit.

You'd go for about two miles in trees and never touch the ground. You'd use your toggle rope, which is a rope you hang round your waist. It goes over your shoulders, round your waist, and it's got an eye on one side and a toggle on the other end. And they fasten that together and you can make a bridge, climbing ropes, anything you like. And they'd make bridges and you'd go up in the trees and you'd swing from one to the other. You'd make a bridge to cross to another one.

And when you got to the top of the hill, you had what they call a death slide. It was a big slide across a gorge. There was quite a few badly injured when I was there, and apparently one or two got killed. There was live ammunition going off everywhere and you had to slide down this wire rope, right across this gorge. If you let go, you'd had it.

Ted's proficiency in exercises in the mountains led to a Sergeant dubbing him 'Taffy, the Welsh goat'. It was a nickname which stuck throughout his training. At the end of his training, Ted was personally presented with his green beret by Lord Lovat.

80 years on, very few people have heard of the World War Two Royal Navy Beach Commandos, an elite group of just 3,000 tough frontline personnel originally formed following Churchill's instructions in 1942. Their purpose was to establish, maintain and control beachheads during amphibious operations, with the essential task of quick and safe turnaround of all boats on the beaches. Archie Thomas from Port Talbot arrived at Achnacarry as a Beach Commando.

I thought I would never do it – ten stone I was, but I did it all. While we there, it was all live ammunition. Six of you on a small boat coming down the river and we were told where to pull in. But before we could get there, they were throwing hand grenades in the water – 'Whoosh', the real thing. And when we were pulling into land, who was facing us – the Sergeant Major and a Sergeant Williams who had been a policeman from Cardiff. Both big fellows with machine-guns. "Spread out." "Get down! Get down!" We could see the tracers going over our heads and they were in between you. That was Achnacarry.

There were three of us from Port Talbot [in the Royal Navy Beach Commandos]: Jim Clegg, Jack Ball and myself. I knew one from Swansea and one from Pembroke, and the boys from the Valleys, I knew them all.

In 2025, at 101 years old, Archie was the last surviving Royal Navy Beach Commando, this rare crack force summoned by the Prime Minister himself, which existed only during World War Two.

Army

The Army was the least prepared for war of Britain's armed forces. Until early 1939, the focus had been on the coastal defence of the British Isles rather than sending an expeditionary force to Europe, with the result that just six months ahead of the outbreak of World War Two, the British Army lacked modern weaponry and mechanised equipment. Then, in March 1939, the Cabinet woke up to the fact that the Army might need to fight on the continent and plans were put in place for the Territorial Army to double in size. By April, conscription was introduced. This push for rapid and massive expansion came far too late, leaving the Army ill-equipped to meet the might of the German military as the Germans pushed through the Low Countries and into France.

Teenager Syd Daw was working in the East Moors steel works and serving in the Home Guard, but he was ready to join the Army. He went along to the recruiting office with a friend named Cliff Murrow, whose family had a shop in Ely.

> The recruiting Sergeant said, "I know where they want fellows like you. The Black Watch are looking for men like you. Blah-blah-blah." And we thought, 'Oh, that sounds interesting.' So off we went. It was February [1943]. Just after my 18th birthday.

Syd and Cliff left Cardiff on a train at 8 p.m. and arrived in Perth, Scotland, at 8 a.m. the next morning.

Having been transferred from the RAF to the Army in August 1944, Duncan Hilling, from Saundersfoot, had been ordered to report to Britannia Barracks in Norwich, spending six weeks there for rifle and bayonet training "and the other bits and pieces".

> From Britannia Barracks in Norwich we went to Brecon, with what was then the Welch Regiment. I spent a lot of time there, climbing up the Beacons, as they liked to get us fit.
>
> After six weeks there, I did something which I was advised never to do, but I am glad I did. They were looking for volunteers to drive vehicles, so I volunteered, and they sent me to Windermere, to train on Bren Gun Carriers – which is a track vehicle, specialising in 6-inch mortars and Bren guns.
>
> Again, I was there for six weeks and thoroughly enjoyed it. From there they sent me back to Wales, this time to Crickhowell to learn how to use Bren Gun Carriers during attacks, and I had six weeks there and then one week near Llandeilo.

Like Duncan, Syd did six weeks of infantry training, before about fourteen weeks of training on a Bren Gun Carrier. "And that's how I learned to drive, in fact," he said.

> There were about sixty of us and the top four were told that they would have a three-week course on motorbikes. I thought, 'Oh, I'd love to do that!' And, luckily, I was one of the four. We were driving around Scotland then in the summer of '43. Brilliant. I thought, 'Oh, what a life this is,' you know.

Syd's unit was due to go to North Africa but about 30 of them were transferred to the 52nd (Lowland) Division, Syd among them. Syd headed to Grantown-on-Spey, on the edge of the Cairngorms.

> We weren't heading to the desert any more. In fact, we were learning to ski with Norwegians to go to Norway. This was

really hard mountain training. Oh gosh, when I think back on it! But there you go, that hardens you up, makes a man of you. And when you went abroad, you realised that it's easier abroad than it was in the training area!

While at a weapons show at Fort George near Inverness, Syd was recruited for a new role.

I was on the end rink firing at a target 200 yards away. I'd got seven shots: two warmers to warm the barrel – and you can use them for firing at the target – and the five at the target. And my two warmers went in the bull, and then my five shots went in the bull. So it was: "Take this soldier's name, Sergeant Major!" Next thing, there's a notice on the board forming a sniper section, and I'm on it! Everyone was saying, "Wait till you get abroad! Snipers don't last five minutes!" And I said, "This one will. I'm not up any trees! You won't find me up a tree looking down. I'll keep away from that."

The dangers of training were continually present throughout the war and across the services, claiming many lives in Wales as well as of Welsh men and women called to arms training elsewhere in the UK and overseas. As Duncan Hilling recalled:

We took a group of six Bren gun vehicles in a line. We carried small bombs and the vehicle would stop quickly and a chap would throw a bomb out of the back, before we returned to our base. On this particular occasion, one of these bombs, which was a phosphorus bomb ended up in a vehicle close by and badly burned a young fellow. I remember this vividly as his face, chest and arms were badly burned but fortunately there was a stream running nearby and we held him under this water for around ten minutes, before the ambulance arrived.

We also learned to use a small plastic bomb. We would run in a line and throw these bombs in front of us, where they would explode, and run back again. One chap collapsed and a ball bearing which set off the bomb, about the size of a marble, hit him in the thigh and shattered his thigh. They stopped doing that afterwards.

Lots of dreadful accidents happened and I can remember one when we were in Windermere, and we were learning about 'sticky' bombs which you dropped on to a tank. We were about 20 feet down a cliff with a disused tank, and pulled the lever off the side of the bomb and dropped it onto the tank, and then went back while it exploded. But we had one boy who decided he would throw it. He pulled the lever and put it behind his neck to throw it and it stuck to his back, and you only have seconds before it detonates, and the Sergeant just pushed him over the top and he was blown up on the way down. Absolutely hideous.

These dreadful accidents happened in the Army and they are very seldom mentioned, but it is something you learn to live with.

6

The Dark Years

"We could see the planes going off and very often we could stay there and try and count them as they came back. And so often they didn't all come back. It was very upsetting because you got to know them, some of the pilots."

PAULINE PENROSE

IN EARLY SEPTEMBER 1940, and by now just turning 18 years old, RAF radio operator Dennis Tidswell was posted to RAF Duxford, home to Douglas Bader's 'Big Wing'.

I found myself stationed in Duxford at the actual time of the Battle of Britain. Duxford was in 12 Group, which looked after the air operations and control of the air space above the Midlands. Below it was 11 Group, and both Groups worked in close cooperation.

In those days, the medium- and long-wave transmissions were very noisy, crackly and mushy, and not easy to understand. But very high-frequency broadcasting was almost like a telephone as we know it today. So my job as a radio operator was to operate the equipment with air traffic (as we called it) between the aircraft and the Ground Control Room.

To explain: the radio operator was at the back of the Control Room, and the Control Room consisted of a plotting board with WAAF lady plotters, a senior RAF officer controller, alongside him was an Army officer and I have a vague recollection of a Naval presence. Anyway, behind all this, maintaining the air traffic conversation and recording it, were the radio operators.

I spent a couple of months there during the Battle of Britain and can remember the dog fights up above. Duxford itself was bombed and was damaged, but I would not describe it as being heavily bombed – at least not as I was to experience later in my RAF career, when I spent most of the war on a different branch of radio operating on the island of Malta.

Tony Bird's school had been evacuated to Lampeter in 1939, living and being taught in what are today the university buildings. In the summer, he and fellow pupils huddled around the wireless in anticipation of the latest reports from the Battle of Britain:

> I think I was about 16 or 17 at the time when the Battle of Britain took place and we [pupils] would follow the course of the battle on the radio. I always remember a marvellous score by the RAF of 183 German aircraft shot down, which turned out to be a little on the high side. But all the boys were cheering and we were very chuffed!

Pauline Penrose remembered the Battle of Britain and watched dogfights overhead before herself being conscripted into the WAAFs, becoming one of the WAAF plotters mentioned by Dennis Tidswell. Pauline was posted further south than Duxford, serving in 11 Group's frontline fighter stations, first at Hornchurch and then North Weald. In peacetime, she had been a draughtswoman, with a special talent for technical drawing and art – skills which were quickly spotted at these RAF stations.

I did all the work that came in, painting the plaques which used to go around the Ops Room, hung on a rail, of all the different squadrons that came. I had to put the squadron number [on the plaques] – 321, or whatever it was. Of course, they were always changing so that meant repainting them.

We had our mess right on the edge of the airfield [North Weald] and we could see the planes going off and very often we could stay there and try and count them as they came back. And so often they didn't all come back. It was very upsetting because you got to know them, some of the pilots.

There were so many squadrons there and these were always changing. We had a Polish one there. All the Poles were tall and slender and quite elegant, and they liked to press their uniforms a certain way, very particular.

Having served at RAF Duxford during the Battle of Britain, Dennis Tidswell was posted to Cranwell, where he qualified as a VHF-DF (Very High Frequency-Direction Finding) operator and waited for his call-up for aircrew training. From Cranwell, Dennis was posted in November 1940 to RAF Kirton in Lindsey, Lincolnshire, where he got into a spot of bother.

I see according to my record it reads 'accepted for training as Pilot, Observer, Wireless Op/AG' on 8/5/1941. So from that date onward I was waiting to go on to aircrew training. But then out of the blue in Kirton in Lindsey along comes this Sergeant and says, "Report to so-and-so as you're being posted abroad." Well now, I couldn't go abroad as I was waiting for aircrew training.

"You're being posted abroad."

"I would like an interview with the Commanding Officer."

"You're being posted abroad."

So I thought, 'To hell with this.'

So I took it into my head to go straight up to the Commanding Officer's office. Leading Aircraftman Tidswell goes into the Station Commander's office and says, "I want to see the Station Commander."

Whereupon I was pounced upon by two Sergeants, who took me one arm either side, knocked my cap off, and frog-marched me backwards out of the office. Then I found myself on a charge for insubordination. So the following day, I appeared in front of the Station Commander. I offered my apologies and said that I was listed for aircrew training so why was I being sent abroad?

He said, "We too have to do as we are told. You, I understand, are a radio VHF-DF operator and wherever you are going, they seem to be urgently needed. So I am sorry, but you are going abroad and, were it not for that fact, you would be on a very serious charge and now you would be spending your time in the glasshouse."

Following Operation Barbarossa, the German invasion of the Soviet Union in June 1941, Britain and Russia signed an agreement for convoys to deliver essential supplies to the Soviet Union via the ports of Archangel (Arkhangelsk) and Murmansk. The Arctic convoys commenced in August 1941. They were fraught and highly dangerous journeys for Merchant Navy shipping and its Royal Navy escorts.

Oliver Lindsay from Barry went to sea on the steamer SS *Botavon*, a supply ship transporting vital cargo to Russia. *Botavon* left Middlesbrough on 31 March 1942 and headed for Murmansk via Reykjavík. Oliver, known as Olly, turned 17 a couple of weeks into the difficult voyage. Then *Botavon* came under air attack.

I was firing a real gun – you know, this wasn't a toy. This was something real. Six torpedo bombers, Heinkel 111s, came in very, very low, just skimming the top of the water. We're firing on these planes coming in. Of course, all the other ships in the convoy, about twenty-odd, were all firing at the planes. And we were in the middle, so we were getting the flak from both sides. Two torpedoes come in just below the water: you could see them drop off the plane. We were firing at the plane as the plane came over, and because they were so low, they had to bank to clear the foremast. And as they were right ahead, I was looking over the gun and I could see the pilot looking at his port engine and his port engine was all on fire. And he crashed just beyond the convoy. But two torpedoes had been launched and they both hit home. I was one of the lucky ones who got into a lifeboat.

Olly was picked up by an armed trawler in the convoy and continued to Murmansk.

Following his brush with the Station Commander at RAF Kirton in Lindsey in the spring of 1941 and the severe reprimand which followed, Dennis Tidswell was indeed posted overseas. He recalled:

I found myself boarding a train for Greenock, and on the train we were really like sardines in a tin. Packed, packed, packed. It was quite an unpleasant journey really. At Greenock we went aboard various ships. Around 1,750 personnel, mainly Army but with about 300 Royal Air Force.

We boarded a ship called the *Leinster*. It turned out to be the smallest in the convoy in which we found ourselves. She just weighed 4,300 tons, whereas a larger merchant ship would be almost 11,000 tons.

We slept in hammocks, which were all slung between various loads of pipes that there are on ships. And one would look and see this line of hammocks swinging away. Now a hammock is a bit tricky to get into on land but on a rolling ship it tends to be very tricky, and the *Leinster* did roll. She didn't have any stabilisers and we were at this time manoeuvring into a convoy. After the war, I looked up the records, which say we were to relieve Malta – Malta at that time being under siege. The 'powers that be' said that this convoy must get through.

During this time, one of our radio operators was a man called Dick Watson, who was from Jamaica and had come over to the UK at his own expense just to join the Royal Air Force. I had great respect for him. He fell somehow and injured his ankle. In the ship's medical quarters they put on a light plaster. He could just hobble around but he needed to be assisted getting in and out of his hammock. However, we are now in our tropical gear with an inordinate number of white knees, and we're heading south...

All of a sudden there was an enormous bang, and the ship shook. It didn't completely turn on its side but was over at a bit of an angle. It leaned onto the port side, I think it was. Bearing in mind it was 80 years ago, I'm a bit vague on detail – but we were down below, a couple of decks down, and we found ourselves in almost complete darkness. There wasn't a chink of light coming through and the gangways and stairways were at a bit of an angle.

Obviously in the almost dark this was a rather frightening situation, given that you were trapped down below with certainly no easy route of access to get out on to deck. And we also had Dick Watson with his injured ankle. Anyway, we could hear a lot of noise, banging and bumping up on the main deck. When we eventually did get through into daylight, the whole place was pandemonium really. I got onto the port side because it didn't seem possible to launch lifeboats on the starboard side, but I never heard the order to abandon ship. But that was clearly what was being done because when you got down to the ship's rail, there were seven lifeboats. Six of them absolutely chocka full and the seventh pretty well full. So they got Dick Watson aboard the lifeboat.

From the ship's rail, I then jumped into the stern part of the last lifeboat. It was a distance of about six or seven feet and you go down with a bit of a bump. Anyway, I was in the stern end of the tightly packed lifeboat. The lifeboats were all put in a line and were connected by a line and the one lifeboat had an engine.

Dennis, quite unofficially, carried a Box Brownie camera with him for the duration of the war.

Next thing we know, out of the mist comes the Rock of Gibraltar. I had my pocket camera in my pocket and to this day I have some photographs which I took from the lifeboat of the Rock of Gibraltar.

At Gibraltar, Dennis and the others were transferred to a warship, HMS *Hermione*.

At this time Malta was under siege, undergoing very heavy bombing. When we went aboard the *Hermione*, we slept against the side of the ship's hull. You slept where you could and kept your tin hat and respirator handy.

I didn't realise it, but at the tip of the boat I suppose I was about to receive my baptism of fire and realise the real horrors of war. On board the *Hermione*, you could volunteer for duties. So having had the experience of being down below when the ship went down off Gibraltar, I didn't fancy the idea of bombing or torpedo raids when I was down below. So I volunteered to work on deck and so I found myself passing boxes of ammunition to the crew gunner of the 'pom-pom' guns. I suppose we were about two days out and the ship was travelling quite fast – with 7,000 tons going along at 32 miles an hour, you know you are moving.

Suddenly the klaxon goes: 'Action Stations, Action Stations'. I hadn't really had time to get up on deck before 'Stand by to Ram, Stand by to Ram', and there was a terrific crash and the ship shuddered from bow to stern, and then carried on sailing. It turned out it had rammed an Italian submarine which was charging its batteries at dawn on the surface, and the following ships in our wake had made contact with the sub underneath their hulls and the *Hermione* had sustained a gash in its bow. But I suddenly realised: what a terrible way to die, being rammed by another ship. That's what I mean when I say the horrors of war became apparent to me.

The date was 2 August 1941 and the action which Dennis had just witnessed became the subject of a well-known wartime propaganda poster, painted by the artist Marcus Stone. The Italian submarine *Tembien* had been cut in two and its Captain, the highly experienced Guido Gozzi, four officers and 37 ratings all perished. *Hermione* suffered only minor damage. Dennis continues:

We were approaching the real hotspots of the passage to the Sicilian straits, and of course in Sicily we had the German Luftwaffe and the Italian Aeronautica. The Italians did their dive-bombing from high level, but they were very accurate, really. The Germans had their [Junkers] Ju 88s and their Stukas [Junkers Ju 87s], and we were coming to well within their range. I had volunteered of course in assisting with passing the ammunition boxes to the pom-pom guns on the deck. The klaxons sounded 'Action Stations' and that was my real baptism of fire, because we came under air attack – mainly bombs falling all around, fortunately missing the ship. I think most had been doing a sort of zigzag course and the ship never stayed still. The angle seemed to alter all the time and the noise was absolutely terrific. The engine noise as the ship was doing its full 32 knots, the exploding shells, bombs, anti-aircraft. It was absolute pandemonium.

However, to comment on my feelings at that time: first of all when it all started, it was one of fright, certainly one of fright. And then suddenly it becomes one of excitement; and then suddenly one of aggression because you then realise it's either him or it's me. You are either going to live or you are going to die. So you had to make every endeavour to survive. It was a feeling I probably never had again, and it is quite an experience really. But anyway, we survived that unscathed and eventually, not very long afterwards, sailed into Malta harbour and tied up.

Less than a year later, *Hermione* was herself sunk by a German submarine off the coast of Egypt, with the loss of 8 officers and 80 ratings.

On the ground in Malta

Having arrived in Malta in August 1941, Dennis spent nearly three years there and on the neighbouring island of Gozo.

We arrived in Malta, disembarked and then we boarded a number of very old, dilapidated buses with no windows. We all looked a little bit like coal miners coming off shift, in that we were dirty and dishevelled. And then we were transported to a place called Safi. Safi Strip was a nice long aircraft runway, large enough to allow Wellington bombers to land, and it was a base mainly for Wellington bombers and Hurricane fighters. We had a tremendous respect for the pilots, because if they didn't use a torpedo on a sortie and they came in to land with a torpedo under the fuselage, then one false move and that would have been curtains. The Safi strip became the Luqa main airport...

For the time being, we had to sleep in the open. There were no washing facilities, we were just being fed. So we then had to take out our billy cans and take out our irons [cooking and eating implements], and we slept in the open for I think it was three nights altogether, before we got back to base at Luqa, and we were able to have normal washing and toiletry facilities.

The wireless mechanics built us radio operators a new VHS/DF high-frequency direction-finding station on the edge of the runway, and it was disguised in an old farm building. And there we operated a watch system and to get back to base we had to walk across the runway.

I can remember one particular time crossing the runway and an Italian Macchi fighter decided to strafe the runway. I was fortunately close to Nellie the steamroller and I dived under the front roller, and that really did save my life. Nearby, about 100 yards or so, was a Wellington bomber which the strafe had set on fire, and luckily for me I got away with that one. The story of Nellie is that Nellie was an old-fashioned steamroller with a big front roller and iron rear wheels and the Wellington bombers would be out bombing the North African coast and in the meantime the Luftwaffe would be bombing Safi. So before the Wellingtons could land from their return journey on the runway, all the bomb holes had to be filled up. It was a case of every hand on deck, filling up the potholes and Nellie the steamroller would iron them out as best it could, to enable the returning aircraft to land.

Iori Lewis of the 146th (Pembroke and Cardiganshire) Field Regiment had joined up when the war began. In June 1942, he and his unit boarded a train at Liverpool. They didn't know their final destination, but most assumed it was India.

It turned out to be Egypt.

We had KD: khaki drill – shorts and pith helmet, which I never wore. And once we landed, we picked up our guns, vehicles, and went out into the desert, to get accustomed to the conditions that we would fight under. Then we joined the 7th Armoured Division – the Desert Rats – which was a great honour, because they were regular units, and we were civilians in uniform – a TA unit, Territorial unit, and we fought with the 7th Armoured.

My first impressions of Egypt and the desert? It was hot, then cold at night – freezing cold at night. Bad food. Corned beef, most of the time, and biscuits. Never saw bread. The biggest thing was the flies – flies everywhere. In their thousands. They used to go in your tea, on your food. And you had to be very careful: there was a lot of illness. Hepatitis B, jaundice, and desert sores. I was very fortunate. I looked out for myself and I didn't suffer anything at all.

The unit's first action was a battle which was to go down in history: El Alamein.

Also in North Africa was 19-year-old pilot Hugh 'Jimmy' James from Cilfynydd, near Pontypridd. Just like Dennis Tidswell, Jimmy had lied about his age to join the RAF.

In August 1942, based in Cairo and tasked with flying supplies across the Western Desert, Jimmy – by then a pilot with 216 Squadron – was instructed to transport 14 wounded troops (and their medics) for treatment. While waiting to take off in the lumbering Bristol Bombay, he was informed that he was to receive another passenger. This special passenger was 44-year-old Lieutenant General William 'Strafer' Gott, who had been ordered to Cairo for a meeting with Winston Churchill. Gott was about to be made the new Commander of the 8th Army in North Africa. Speaking years later on *Wings Over Wales* (HTV Wales), Jimmy recalled that, just 15 minutes into the flight...

...two Messerschmitt Bf 109s shot past me. As they went away, I shouted, "Let's pull up." As I was doing so, I was attacked again by two more and they absolutely filled the aircraft with shells. There was absolute chaos, and they were aiming for certain to cripple us forever. And then when they had finished, a third pair came along, so there were six aircraft altogether and they were obviously quite determined to destroy us.

With remarkable skill, Jimmy managed to land the aircraft, cascading along the rough terrain until it came to a halt.

> As I came around in the crashed wings and the chaos, there in front of me were just four people [alive] and until that moment, I didn't know that I had been wounded or touched. I was badly wounded in the back, my leg was hanging off and my hands were burnt down to the bones, but I didn't know anything about it. Instead of the 21 people who had been on board, there were just four left. It was absolutely heartbreaking, a terrible shock.

Lieutenant General Gott was dead. Despite his own severe injuries and under protest from the other survivors, Jimmy determined that it was his responsibility to go for help. He crawled seven miles across the desert before being rescued by a Bedouin tribesman, who tied him on the back of his camel and rode to the British. It was an extraordinary feat of courage, determination and resilience.

> Normally one fighter could have put us down, so there was no need for six. It was a deliberate attack to kill General Gott, who was the one General Rommel was concerned about. This was their game plan.

But in war there are two sides to every story and this one is no exception. Emil Clade, of JG27 'Afrika', was the leader of the Luftwaffe-*Schwarm* of aircraft which had attacked the Bristol Bombay. Interviewed for the 1996 book *Combat Kill*, he said:

> I shot down Lieutenant General Gott, who was on his way to assume command of the 8th Army at Cairo. His aircraft was attacked by my *Schwarm*.
> I waited until the latter's aircraft was over the desert and then dived down on him with four fighters. As I was the

leader of this *Schwarm*, I was able to fire on him first. He was flying at a height of 20 to 30 metres. They felt so secure that they had not even occupied the rear gun pod. My fire was effective on the engine and the pilot immediately reduced the power in order to land, which was no problem in the desert. Meanwhile, my remaining three fighters came in after me, also firing.

After the General's aircraft had landed, the crew started to jump out of the aircraft, although it was rolling along. No, Gott did not die through my gunfire, but by jumping out of the rolling aircraft and breaking his neck. I still have one living witness for this event, the other two having died in the war.

Remarkably, Emil and Jimmy would meet in 2005, and it appears from accounts of the meeting that there was both mutual respect and a genuine warmth between the former adversaries.

But their earlier 'meeting' in 1942 proved to be one of the most significant moments of the war for, with Gott dead, Churchill was forced to find an alternative Commander for the 8th Army in North Africa. His choice was General Bernard Montgomery, quickly to become better known as 'Monty'.

Serving in the 8th Army at this time was Lance Bombardier George Roberts from Aberystwyth. George had already seen considerable action since the beginning of the war and after North Africa was to join the 5th Army in Italy, before fighting his way through France and Germany post D-Day.

George then returned to Aberystwyth to marry his sweetheart Mary, who herself had served in the ATS, bringing home with him a precious handwritten speech given by Montgomery to his 8th Army troops in March 1943, which George had carried with him since leaving North Africa (see photo section).

7

The Tide Turns

"Beth yffach y'ch chi'n neud yma?"
[What the hell are you doing here?]
NEVILLE BOWEN

IN 1942, HAVING gained a reputation as being rather useful
with a shotgun and become an unofficial provider of rabbit
and game, harvested from the fields around Lampeter, Tony
Bird volunteered for the Royal Navy. After initial training…

…I was then sent to join a ship which was just being refitted
in Harland & Wolff's Yard in Belfast – HMS *Escapade*. We
were a completely new crew, the ship having been extensively
refitted after many very difficult Arctic convoys.

We did some Atlantic convoys and were then detailed to
accompany a huge fleet of ships going down to North Africa
for Operation Torch, which was a joint American/British
invasion of North Africa. We escorted HMS *Furious*, the
aircraft carrier which was taking this pretty rough trip, going
down from the Bay of Biscay. I always remember Seafires
taking off from her deck – the deck must have been at angles
of fifteen to twenty degrees. How the pilots ever got the
things down, I don't honestly know.

During one Atlantic convoy we needed oil so we proceeded
to the Azores – with the Azores being Portuguese owned and
neutral territory – and we oiled. I recall the ship being loaded

up with a tremendous amount of pineapple, to keep us going for about ten days until we got back to harbour in the UK. Having oiled, we left the Azores about midday. As we were leaving, to our amazement a German U-Boat was entering the harbour and the officers on our and their boat saluted each other, and all the ratings were waving at each other. We were quite astounded but, of course, we realised that with the island being neutral, it could accommodate warships of any nation and that's what occurred. It was a unique experience and it made me think how futile war was, because here we were waving to people who the next day would like to blow us out of the water.

Aged 18, Archie Thomas had been quickly recruited into the elite Royal Navy Beach Commandos. After training, he became a member of 'Nan' (or 'N') Commando, a unit consisting of 70 men which was split into three sections. Archie was in 'N2', commanded by Lieutenant Maurice Redshaw. The two other Port Talbot boys, Jack Ball and Jim Clegg, were in 'O' Commando and 'R' Commando respectively.

On 28 June 1943, 'N' Commando set sail from the Clyde to take part in Operation Husky, the Allied invasion of Sicily. On the night of 9/10 July, N2 were on 'Green Beach' near the Sicilian town of Pachino. Six days later, they moved to 56 Beach, Portopalo, just a few miles away. N2 ensured that the invasion landing craft got onto the beaches, discharged their troops and machinery of war and then got off the beach as quickly as they could, to return to the host ship to load up again and repeat.

On 25 July, 'N' Commando were shipped from Sicily to Malta, arriving the following day. They witnessed an attack on the aircraft carrier HMS *Indomitable* in the Grand Harbour and then made a quick getaway from Malta, arriving at Oued Marsa, near Bougie (now Béjaïa) in Algeria, and meeting up with the British 4th Army Division.

With some wishful thinking, at that point 'N' Commando thought they might be about to go home. Instead, they found themselves back in Catania, Sicily, via Egypt.

We heard then that we were going to do the raid on Italy. We were in a lemon grove during the day, then at night the Petty Officer called out, "Come on, let's have you! Fall in three deep!" Down to the landing craft – half past four in the morning – straight across the Messina Straits to Gallico Marina, and that's where I caught it…

Archie looked up to see three Junkers Ju 87 'Stuka' dive-bombers, single-engine aircraft notorious for their unique ability to dive vertically as they dropped their bombs. Mounted on each aircraft were sirens known as 'Jericho trumpets', which created a high-pitched screaming noise as the plane dived, maximizing terror in those on the ground.

Shrapnel from the exploding bombs punctured Archie's left thigh and knocked him off his feet. A pal put out a hand to try to help him. But Archie then saw that his friend had been hit by shrapnel in the stomach and chest. Fatally injured, the other man fell back. Still on the ground, Archie noticed that blood was quickly welling up in his thigh and travelling down to his boot.

I was put on a stretcher and taken into the Red Cross tent. The siren was going again and a chap came over and gave me a pillow: "Here, put this over your head." They then took us back over the Messina Straits on landing craft. I don't know if it was a church they took us into in the night, but I could feel them buggering about with my leg and then they shipped us off to the hospital, 46 General. But they didn't do much for me and I have still got the shrapnel here [pointing to his thigh]… small pieces.

Archie was transferred to the hospital ship *Leinster* and taken to a field hospital in Bizerte. Following a two-week stay, he was discharged and taken to Djidjeli (Jijel) in Algeria, to a transit camp called HMS *Hamilcar*.

Also involved in the invasion of Italy in September 1943 was Iori Lewis, by now of the 7th Armoured Division. He was in charge of four guns being transported into Salerno on an LCT (Landing Craft, Tank) – an amphibious vehicle for landing tanks on beachheads. Iori's landing was a precarious and slightly ignominious one.

> I thought the landing craft had stopped about a quarter mile from the shore, so I went on deck to see what was happening. There was quite a battle going on. Some of the LCTs were on fire because we were observed by the Germans. And all of a sudden, the LCT captain opened up the boat and rammed the beach. I was on top deck. So I dashed down three flights of stairs, I caught the last gun going through, I sort of jumped on the barrel of the gun, put my arms around the barrel, then my legs around the barrel. And I landed at Salerno soaking wet with water. If I hadn't got off then, I often wonder, because the LCT pulled out immediately after the last gun and I'd have been back in Tripoli with a court martial – would it be a 'failure to abandon ship'?

Iori and his guns fought their way up past Vesuvius to Naples.

> We finished up in Monte Cassino, which was a terrible place to be in, up to your ankles in mud all the time. Slippery mud. But we were very lucky: we had very few casualties – some wounded, but no-one killed at all.

The rocky slopes and hilltop monastery at Cassino had become a key part of a line of defences which the Germans believed would stop the Allies getting any further northwards. The monastery, which was being used as a fortress by the Germans, was eventually destroyed by a series of heavy American bombing raids. By then, Iori had been relieved and his unit was on the way back to Britain and a short period of leave. They retrained with new guns, larger teams, and prepared to return to action.

Just a few weeks earlier on 15 August 1943, back in west Wales, Air Training Corps Cadet Duncan Hilling recalled:

> I was working in a shop in Saundersfoot, and quite often would take a shotgun out to shoot rabbits, pigeons to help the food supply. On this particular Wednesday [when shops were usually closed in the afternoon in this period], I watched a Hawker Henley flying overhead, and for me it was travelling much too slow. It passed just about half a mile from me and plunged straight into the ground. I saw the plane come down and mud fly up in the air. The two boys were killed at a farm called Thorney Park and were buried in St Issel's Church, Saundersfoot.

In fact, the 'two boys' referred to by Duncan were both pilots from 595 Squadron, which had recently been formed at RAF Aberporth. Flight Lieutenant Frank Davies (pilot) and Flying Officer John Robertson (passenger) were flying anti-aircraft cooperation duties in their Hawker Henley Mk. III L-3336 aircraft over Mid Wales.

It was generally accepted within RAF circles that to be selected for Special Duties and to fly SOE (Special Operations Executive) agents into occupied territories, an 'above average' rating as a pilot was needed. Reg Pyatt fitted the bill perfectly, for he had often flown into France during the 1930s, knew much of the local terrain, and was particularly adept at flying through any weather conditions. He flew a single-engine high-wing Westland Lysander, often with two agents tightly squeezed into the back seat behind him.

I was what was called a 'dirty weather pilot'. You were doing your part of getting somebody into the enemy's quarters and putting a spoke in the enemy's wheels, so to speak.

Often the local Resistance would light up the landing zone.

I didn't get out of the aircraft. I just landed and they [the agents] got out and the instruction was for them to bang the fuselage when it was clear for me to press the starter. And then I was off like lightning!

In 1944, 20-year-old Eric Evans, born in Banwen in the Neath Valley, was posted to 99 Squadron, which was stationed in RAF Dhubulia, Bengal, India, and equipped with the heavy, four-engined B-24 Liberator. Eric, a bomb-aimer, flew missions over Burma, providing close support to the 14th Army and also "moving big guns" from one location to another for them.

Close to finishing his first operational tour (normally 30 missions), Eric's Liberator attacked Japanese oil tankers at sea off the coast. Flying at just 55 feet above the waves, the aircraft was hit by anti-aircraft fire and badly damaged. The pilot managed to keep the aircraft above sea level until it reached landfall, but eventually the Liberator dived straight into the ground. Eric remembers being "belted around a bit" – which was a bit of an understatement, for he was, in fact, severely injured. After spending several months in hospital, followed by non-flying duties, he was discharged from the RAF.

Flying on ops over Germany, Pembrokeshire-born brothers Doug and John Evans would spend the middle years of the war flying Halifax bombers – although one would be brought down and face a fight for survival behind enemy lines.

Doug had joined the RAF in 1940, first as a flight mechanic and then as a pilot, training in Canada and the USA. He joined 10 Squadron at RAF Melbourne, Yorkshire, in August 1943.

He flew 32 missions in the Handley Page Halifax, his targets mainly in Germany, such as Mannheim and Munich.

The German targets were all big raids – two/three/four hundred aircraft.

On one raid, Doug faced one of the biggest fears of the Bomber Command aircrew: being 'coned' – locked onto – by searchlights over the target.

It was over Mannheim-Ludwigshafen in November of 1943. We were coned over the target after we'd just dropped bombs. The master searchlight got us and that was a purply one – we all recognised that one – and they somehow had some automatic or electronic system hanging on to you, and all the others [searchlights] came round. And so we were the unlucky ones on that occasion.

And having been coned, the tail gunner immediately told me to corkscrew, which was the manner by which we flew the aeroplane to try to get out of the cone or to avoid attack. But, in fact, very shortly after being coned we were attacked by Focke-Wulf 190s. I was descending and corkscrewing from the bombing height of about 17,000 feet. The cone stayed with us down to about 7,000 feet, and we levelled out at 5,000 feet.

The tail gunner claimed that he had shot down one of the two Focke-Wulf 190s that attacked us. We were lucky: we had plenty of hits on our aeroplane, but none of the systems of the aeroplane were damaged in any way and none of us were injured. We came through quite safely. But anyway, we climbed back up very slowly… Everybody was very tense… because you felt so alone climbing back up there. But we got home safely in the end. We were very fortunate, very fortunate.

Neville Bowen from Ammanford served initially on the troop ship *Louis Pasteur*, taking RAF personnel to Canada and the USA. Upon arrival in Halifax, Nova Scotia, Neville was instructed to take a six-day train down to San Francisco to join a merchant ship.

> I was a DEMS [Defensively Equipped Merchant Ship] gunner, which is a Royal Navy gunner attached to a Merchant ship, but before joining the ship in San Francisco I was invited to a hotel to meet a very famous film star called Anna Neagle. I had lunch with her and afterwards met several American dignitaries.

After the Atlantic convoy, they joined a Mediterranean convoy.

> Now, two of my brothers were in the Army: my brother next to me, Doug, and my eldest brother, Will. Doug was in the Welch Regiment and Will was in the Royal Artillery. We left Port Said and travelled to Naples. When we got to Naples, I was on watch on the gangplank and one of the stewards in the port came across and started talking to me. He was English and recognised my Welsh accent and he said, "Hey, some of your boys are here."
> "The Welch Regiment?" I asked.
> He said, "Yeah," so I replied, "Dammit, my brother is in the Welch Regiment. Are they still here, then?"
> "Yes, they're still here!"
> "Right, once I have finished here, I will fetch some of my mates and we will see if we can go and find them."
> Anyway, I finished my watch, and I had one of my mates with me and we were walking down this road in Naples. And about 50 yards ahead I saw this bloke, and ran up to him and tapped him on the shoulder, and he turned around and said to me in Welsh, *"Beth yffach y'ch chi'n neud yma?"* [What the hell are you doing here?]

It wasn't the one I was looking for [in the Welch Regiment], but my eldest brother, Will, who was in the Royal Artillery. So we took him back to the ship and gave him a good meal. And we went out then and had a few drinks. After that I didn't see him again until after the end of the war.

Anyway, we went back to the ship and sailed again, but from the Mediterranean to New York. We loaded up again and went back to the Mediterranean, and this time to Alexandria, and it was in Alexandria I was told that my brother Doug had been wounded at Monte Cassino and he was in the 70th British General Hospital in Naples. I was supposed to come off this ship and return to the UK. I asked, "Where's this ship going next?"

"It's going to Naples," I was told.

"Well, I'll stay on," I said.

So I stayed on the ship and I went to Naples, and I asked when we reached there, "Where's the 70th General Hospital?"

"It's on the bottom of Vesuvius, at a place called Pompeii."

"How do I get there?"

"Go out to the *autostrada* [motorway] and stick your hand up, and one of the trucks will pick you up!"

And, sure enough, I got a lift to this hospital and, when I was there, my brother was there. When I think back it gets to me every time. Anyway, I sat with him for hours and he was in a bad way. I visited him for three days and on the third day I went to see him, and he said, "I've got bad news for you... And I don't know how to tell you."

"What's that?" I said.

"The next hospital ship in, I'm going to go home on it."

"Well, I've got good news for you," I said. "Because the hospital ship is in and I'm going home on it too."

So I left and on the *autostrada* there were two Air Force men.

"Can I get lift from here into Naples?" I said.

One of them turned to me and said, "Well, Neville, what are you doing here?" He was from Saron!

So I had a lift back to Naples and from there we sailed back to the Atlantic and back home. Now, when we were on the journey back, we were in this convoy and again, I am saying how lucky we were, because there were ships on the other side of the convoy being torpedoed, and the next thing the ship in front of us was torpedoed. And we were pulling out to pass this ship, and there was a man who had been blown off the ship and into the sea. And you know, we couldn't do anything about it. We couldn't stop to pick him up, but we knew that there were Royal Navy ships, and they were supposed to pick up survivors. After that I was on watch, and I saw a torpedo passing our ship. How? God only knows, because I don't.

When we got back to this country, my brother was brought back by taxi, accompanied by a nurse, all the way back to Swansea Hospital, and so I started visiting him there. He started getting better.

Both my brothers came home and my other brother [Will, in the Royal Artillery] was also unscathed.

8

Evasion

"Believe me, when you're on your own, you really feel
on your own. You can't believe it's happened to you; it's
something that, you know, happens to other people.
I could hear the bombers above returning to the bases
and their breakfasts and a little rum or something like
that. And I thought, 'You lucky so-and-sos… Here am I!'"

GEORGE DUFFEE

GEORGE DUFFEE, WHO had lied about his age to get his
pilot's wings at the age of just 18, found that his luck ran out
very quickly. It was 22 June 1943.

In Bomber Command, you had to go with an experienced
crew for one trip as co-pilot. And this was my one trip. This
was my first operational trip against a target in Germany.
And on the way back, we were coned by searchlights.
And believe me, everything you read about searchlights is
absolutely true: you feel like you're naked in Piccadilly.

And then, of course, a night fighter, which was an Me
110 [Messerschmitt Bf 110], was underneath us, which is a
blind spot for a Halifax – there's no bubble underneath [for
a gunner] like on a Flying Fortress, for example. And he shot
us. They normally aimed for the engines and the fuel tanks.

And I was standing by the captain, Flight Lieutenant
Knight, for the first trip in Bomber Command. And all I

could see were these 20 mm shells pounding on the starboard engines, which quickly went in flames, and eventually the wing came off.

But by then I was out… We started off at 18,000 feet and I was actually 'ejected', I would say, from the aeroplane because, you know, forces were pinning you down. I finally got out at about 1,500 feet and arrived, thankfully, in Holland. We'd just crossed the border. We were in Holland. And that's where it all started. My evasion.

Pembrokeshire-born brothers Doug and John Evans were both in the air during the spring of 1944, on missions deep into the heart of Germany. Both flew Halifax bombers.

Doug remembered:

In the main, my early operations had been on German targets. But then we did some of the softening up of targets prior to D-Day in the months of April and May. I think I did about five or six in Belgium, France, targets of that kind – interspersed with continuing German targets too.

In April 1944, John arrived with 158 Squadron at RAF Lissett, near Bridlington, joining a crew whose pilot had been killed.

Our first raids were attacks on marshalling yards and similar areas in France and Belgium which would be helpful to the Germans running up to the invasion. I only did two operations over German targets, Düsseldorf and Karlsburg, and they were a different kettle of fish altogether. Going into Düsseldorf, I remember a huge wall of searchlights – it was like flying into daylight in a way, or even worse than that – and a terrific amount of anti-aircraft fire, of course, as well as night-fighters. I mean, the Ruhr was an important target and it was always well defended. So that was quite an ordeal really, and Karlsburg similarly.

But it was on a raid over Belgium that John's luck ran out. It was the night of 12/13 May 1944, John's twelfth mission.

We were attacking marshalling yards at Hasselt in northern Belgium. We had only just dropped our bombs and were about to set off for home when we were attacked, and you could feel the cannon shells coming through – you could hear it. The aeroplane filled up with smoke, fire broke out, the controls went and wouldn't answer, so I gave the order to bale out.

The gunners had been watching out for fighters, but neither of them saw the Me 110, as it turns out. Of course, they had a habit of coming underneath the plane. They were shielded to some extent: the best place to attack was from below, which presumably is what happened on this occasion. The rear gunner, he could swivel his turret, open the door and drop out. The mid-upper gunner and the engineer, their place of escape in an emergency was the entrance door to the plane, which was on the side, and the rest of us went out the front escape hatch. So I finally went out and I noticed my clip-on parachute was lying very near to the exit to the hatchway, so I quickly grabbed hold of that and snapped it onto the harness and jumped out. The parachute opened with a terrific jerk and I lost one of my flying boots, so I was going down now with just one flying boot.

As I got nearer the ground, I could see this dark area below me and I was fearful it was a lake or water of some sort, but it turned out to be a wood, a forest with very tall trees, and the parachute actually caught the top of these trees. It afforded me quite a gentle drop onto the land. I had no idea where I was, of course. I obviously had to get the parachute down and hide it, somehow or another, to prevent it being seen the following day by reconnaissance planes.

You have your escape kit, of course, which contains a map, some Horlicks tablets, and a compass and that sort of thing, and that is about it really; and then it is up to you, depending on the circumstances of where you have landed and so on. I managed to get the parachute down eventually, making quite a bit of noise – the branches broke, and so on. I dug a shallow hole and buried it. And, of course, there were several hours to go before daylight. I just had to sit there for the time being and think about things.

The first thing was the crew. I was hoping above everything else that they had escaped OK and they were all well. Thankfully, they all were, as it turned out. I was also thinking of my family at home as well. They were going to hear before long that I was missing, get the usual telegram. Then there was my brother, Doug, who was actually flying at this time on operations himself. He had four or five trips to do to complete his tour, so it was a big thing for him to do those five trips as well.

John was now stuck in an occupied land, facing capture or death, not knowing who to trust. Meanwhile, the preparations for D-Day went on without him.

It was in June 1943 when George Duffee jumped from his blazing Halifax over the Netherlands. He spent the first five days on his own. He was lonely and trying desperately to remember everything the RAF intelligence officers had told flying crew like him about how to evade capture.

Believe me, when you're on your own, you really feel on your own. You can't believe it's happened to you; it's something that, you know, happens to other people. I could hear the bombers above returning to the bases and their breakfasts and a little rum or something like that. And I thought, 'You lucky so-and-sos… Here am I!' And so it takes a long, long time to adjust yourself.

But the briefing really said that if there's a crash site, the Germans intensively search in an area of 5 to 10 km on the first night, so you have to walk away from that. I saw the aircraft crash about three miles away.

After walking for five days, George came to a place called Berlicum and spent some time watching a café.

I observed who was going in, who was coming out, and I deduced it would be safe to enter. And then when I entered this cafe, there was a lady there and we had a phrase card which does help. You say something like, *"Ik ben Engels"* – that's in Dutch. But you have to be very wary because you don't quite know who they are at this stage. But the next phrase is something like, *"Ik heb dorst"*: I'm thirsty. So if she offers you some tea, you know she's going to be a friend. And if she offers you a sandwich, which she did, then even better. And then, of course, eventually I said to her through the phrase card, "Can you find someone who speaks English?"

And that was my introduction to the resistance people in Holland. And I cannot emphasise too strongly how wonderful these people were. Because I think without them, many evaders would not have made a home run, as we call it.

But anyway, eventually, she brought a schoolmaster, Martin der Kinderen [of Rosmalen], and he was the beginning of this long, long line of helpers.

But before he got further help, George faced a massive scare. The evasion lines who helped airmen had to be extremely wary of German agents who were passing themselves off as airmen in order to uncover these resistance organisations.

I was actually interrogated at pistol point, not by Martin der Kinderen, but by the local chief of that area. And, unfortunately, I'd just come off leave, and I hadn't got my identity discs – you probably know about these things: you know, 'dog tags', I think the Americans call them – so I had to

sort of convince them and they put it to the vote, because a
lot of these resistance people were infiltrated by bogus pilots,
Polish or Dutch or whatever, to try and put the system out of
order. So it was rather troublesome.

The vote was taken and I won by one vote, which was
Martin der Kinderen. So he's my original helper and my
saviour, in a way.

George Duffee remained free thanks to Dutch and Belgian
people risking their lives to move him towards France.

I had a close encounter at a station in Holland. You're never
actually with your helper, you have to be apart, so that if
you're picked up, which is possible, then your helper is
not picked up at the same time. And I was just waiting on
this platform and a German soldier came along and said,
"Where's the eight-something to Nijmegen?" I could speak a
little bit of Dutch by then, so I said, "Platform nine," which
was the one I was waiting for.

There was a splendid chap called Karst Smit. He was a
Dutch policeman, and he had authority to run a motorcycle.
So I went on this motorcycle across the border into Belgium
and eventually Brussels.

In Brussels, George was handed to the Comet Line, one of
the main organisations helping Allied airmen. This passed air
crew via a string of couriers, escorts and contacts to the south
of France and over the Pyrenees into neutral Spain.

Very often you stayed in what we call 'safe houses',
where there were children. Well, children are naturally
chatterboxes, so if ever they saw you and you couldn't speak
the language, you were a deaf mute or something like that.
Or an uncle just going around the bend.

Once George and his friend Edward, a Canadian air gunner, reached a village just north of Saint-Jean-de-Luz, they could see the Pyrenees, which George called "a beautiful sight, the last barrier" to their freedom. But they weren't safe yet.

A French gendarme got his pistol out and said, *"Halte!"*, and being law-abiding citizens, we stopped. But the others had gone on – the helper and the two other evaders. And he said, "Where are your papers?" We had false papers, which were quite good, saying we were on a bicycle tour from Paris. But he said, "I don't think you're French." Then he said something rather unkind, I thought: "I believe you are German soldiers deserting to Spain because you're fed up with the war."

And so I thought, 'Well, let's go along with that.' I said, "Yes, we're fed up with Mister Hitler. We just want to get over the Pyrenees into Spain." He said, "First of all, you must come with me to the station."

Then I said to Edward in rapid English, so this chap didn't understand, "Let's tell him the truth."

So I said we were a couple of pilots evading to go back to UK, eventually over the Pyrenees to Spain, Gibraltar, etc. And then I touched him on the shoulder – I was near enough to touch him, and I was near enough to punch him, if necessary, because it had taken me four months to get this far! And I said, "We're a couple of pilots going to Spain to carry on the war – *vive la France!*"

He said, "Come with me. We'll have a drink", which was the last thing I wanted to do. So we went to the police station and eventually he brought in all his chums. "Look what I got here. Two pilots going to Spain and Gibraltar to fight the war again!"

Eventually George and Edward were able to make their excuses and find Franco, the guide, to take them over the Pyrenees.

9

Captured

"The crowds on the platform started surging towards us, wanting to get their hands on us. But luckily the German Sergeant in charge of the escort party knew his job very well and immediately pushed us against the wall, and with his men formed a semicircle around us. He made it quite clear that he was going to open fire if these civilians came any nearer."

JOHN MARTIN

RON JONES FROM Newport had been an engineer in a reserved occupation when, in 1940, he received his call-up papers due to a clerical error. By 1942, he was fighting with the Welch Regiment in North Africa.

We got up as far as Benghazi in Libya and then, I think it was about the first or second week in January, we heard that the Germans were out there – Rommel had come out with the Germans. We didn't know how true it was.

So a Sergeant Major said to me one morning, "Corporal Jones, take a section up the road and have a look: see what's happening." So I picked out about ten men and we marched up the road. I think we'd gone about 600 or 700 yards, and there was a big tank coming down the road, with a man standing up in front. When he spotted us, he turned the machine gun on us, and in perfect English he said, "Drop

614 Squadron's Hawker Hectors flying over Cathays Park, Cardiff on Empire Air Day, 20 May 1939.

Archive of No. 614 (County of Glamorgan) Squadron, Royal Auxiliary Air Force

Call-up: at the Talbot Hotel, Tregaron, 1939. From the album of George Roberts.

Nigel Davies

Arthur Morgan's wartime grave, his Fairey Battle canopy lying above him.

Malcolm Hale

C7/563340   15th May 1940.

Dear Sir.

          In confirmation of my telegram of todays date and regret to inform you that your son No 563340 Sergeant Arthur Charles Morgan of No 105 Squadron, Royal Air Force, is missing, the aircraft of whichhe was a member of the crew having failed to return to its base on the 14th of May 1940, after an operational flight.   This does not necessarily mean that he is killed or wounded. You will, of course, be notified immediately when any definate news is received. Should you , in the meantime, receive any further informationregarding your son, from any source, I would appreciate it if you would communicate with me at once.   In conveying this information to you, may I assure you of the sympathy of the Royal Air Force with you in your great anxiety

                I am,
                Dear Sir,
                    Your obedient Servant,
                       D Harris.

E W Morgan Esq
   6 Union St,
     Ammanford   Air Commodore
       Carmarthenshire.   Officer I/C Records,
                       Royal Air Force.

Telegram received by Arthur Morgan's family after he was shot down.
Malcolm Hale

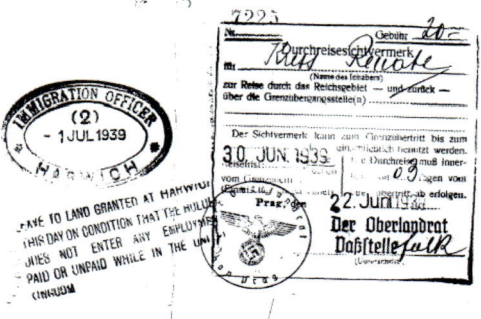

Renate Kress (later Collins)' permit to travel, stamped by German authorities on 30 June 1939 and by British Immigration the next day.

Renate Collins BEM, via WWVA (West Wales Veterans' Archive)

Vera Buchthal (later Stephanie Shirley), right, with her sister, before leaving by Kindertransport.

Dame Stephanie Shirley CH, via WWVA

Renate Collins with Sir Nicholas Winton (seated) on the 70th Anniversary of the Kindertransport from Prague.

Renate Collins BEM, via WWVA

Flight Lieutenant Kemys Morgan, MiD*. 105 Squadron (1939–40); 98 Squadron (1944–5).

David Morgan

Pauline Penrose, WAAF aircraft plotter at Hornchurch and North Weald, was also attached to Air Sea Rescue during the war.

Pauline Penrose, via WWVA

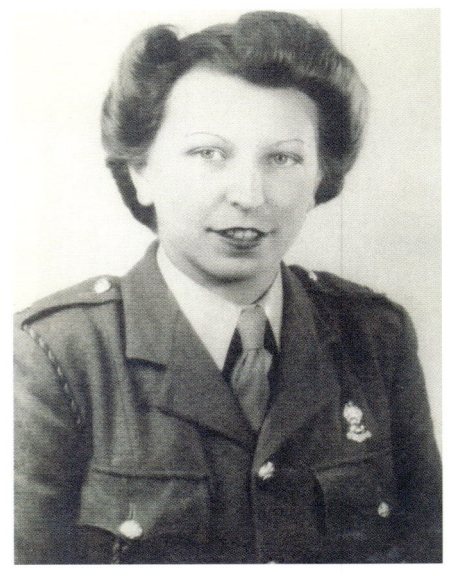

ATS plotter Enid Lewis.

Jane Lewis, via WWVA

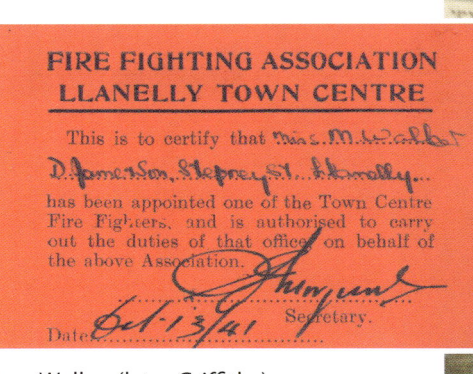

Mary Walker (later Griffiths) was a teenage fire-fighter before becoming a WAAF.

Mary Griffiths, via WWVA

Mary Griffiths at RAF Morecambe Bay, autumn 1942.

Mary Griffiths, via WWVA

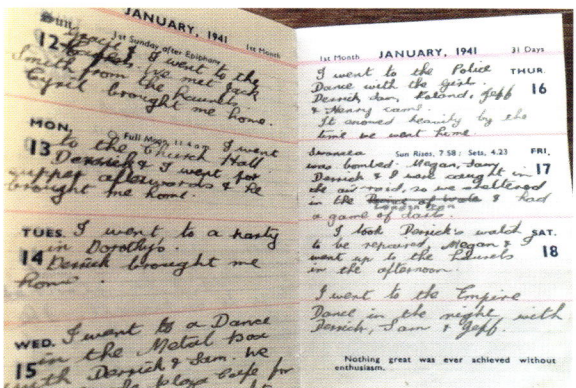

Enid Lewis' diary for 17 January 1941, mentioning the bombing of Swansea.

Jane Lewis, via WWVA

Neville Bowen (RN DEMS gunner) and Ted Owens (Royal Marines Commando) together, 2023.

Pembroke Dock Heritage Centre

Flying Officer Trevor Jones, who featured in the film *Night Bombers*.

Alan & Sian Jones, via WWVA

Royal Welch Fusilier Duncan Hilling in Japan, 1946.

Duncan Hilling, via WWVA

Wren Florence Bird (left), probably off Normandy in late summer 1944.

Jackie Neatherway, via WWVA

Wartime cartoon of Adelaide Jarman with an Airspeed Oxford at RAF Little Rissington.

Adelaide and John Martin, via WWVA

W/Op and POW John Martin and WAAF flight mechanic Adelaide Martin, 2021.

Royal Army Service Corps despatch rider and D-Day veteran Gordon Prime.

Prime family, via WWVA

Personal message from the army commander

1) On 5 March ROMMEL addressed his troops in the mountains overlooking our positions and said that if they did not take MEDENINE, and force the Eighth army to withdraw, then the days of the axis forces in North Africa were numbered.

The next day, 6 March, he attacked the Eighth army. He should have known that the Eighth Army NEVER WITHDRAWS therefore his attack could end only in failure — which it did.

2) We will now show ROMMEL that he was right in the statement he made to his troops.

The days of the axis forces in North Africa are indeed numbered.

The Eighth Army and the Western Desert air force, together constituting one fighting machine, are ready to advance. We all know what that means, and so does the enemy.

3) In the Battle that is now to start, the Eighth Army:

   a) Will destroy the enemy now facing us in the MARETH position,

   b) Will burst through the GABES GAP,

   c) Will then drive Northwards on SFAX, SOUSSE and finally TUNIS

4) We will not stop, or let up, till TUNIS has been captured, and the enemy has either given up the struggle or been pushed into the sea.

5) The operations now about to begin will mark the close of the campaign in North Africa. Once the battle starts the eyes of the world will be on the Eighth army, and millions of people will listen to the wireless every day — hoping anxiously for good news. We must not let them be anxious. Let us see that they get good news, and plenty of it, every day.

If each one of us does his duty, and pulls his full weight, then nothing can stop the Eighth army. And nothing will stop it.

FORWARD TO TUNIS! DRIVE THE ENEMY INTO THE SEA

B L MONTGOMERY
General, GOC in C, Eighth Army

March 1943.

Handwritten speech by General Montgomery to troops in North Africa, March 1943, brought back to Aberystwyth by 8th Army veteran George Roberts.

Nigel Davies

WW2 veterans shooting range event. L–R: Archie Thomas, Duncan Hilling, Neville Bowen, Tony Bird, Idwal Davies – average age 100. Duncan Hilling (98) won with 94/100!

Age Cymru Dyfed

54th Pilots' Course, Grosse Ile, Michigan, 1943. Tony Bird is third from left, front row.

Tony Bird, via WWVA

'Our Greatest Generation' Age Cymru Dyfed event, 2023. L–R: Idwal Davies (Army); Ceredig Evans (Royal Navy); Duncan Hilling (RAF & Army); Neville Bowen (Royal Navy); Lord Lieutenant of Dyfed, Sara Edwards; Veterans' Commissioner for Wales, Col. James Phillips; Tony Bird (Royal Navy); Charlotte 'Betty' Webb MBE (Bletchley Park); Richard Pelzer (Army); Dr Norman Rose (Royal Marines Commando).

Age Cymru Dyfed (Phil Marland)

Portrait of WAAF Corporal Jean McKay painted by an RAF colleague during the war.

WWVA

Dorothy Evans from Tal-y-bont died after a Halifax from 1658 HCU crashed into the WAAF quarters at RAF Fairwood Common on 9 April 1944.

Dennis Tidswell by his VHS-DF set in RAF HQ at Valetta, Malta, c.1943.

Dennis Tidswell, via WWVA

Mobile VHS-DF section led by Dennis Tidswell (standing, third from right), 27 February1945 – minutes before the V1 bomb injury which ended his war.

Dennis Tidswell, via WWVA

Sniper Syd Daw (back left) with members of his unit near the front line in the Netherlands, January 1945.

Syd Daw

John Evans (front left) with the crew that took off in Halifax HX 334 on the night of 12 May 1944.

John Evans

Bomber pilot Doug Evans, who flew 32 missions in his Halifax.

Royal Marines Commando Ted Owens, badly wounded at Sword Beach on D-Day.
Ted Owens

Iori Lewis shortly before taking part in the invasion of Italy, 1943.
Iori Lewis

Bomb-aimer Fred Seal from Barry.
Fred Seal

Glyn James in Kinmel Bay, 2012.

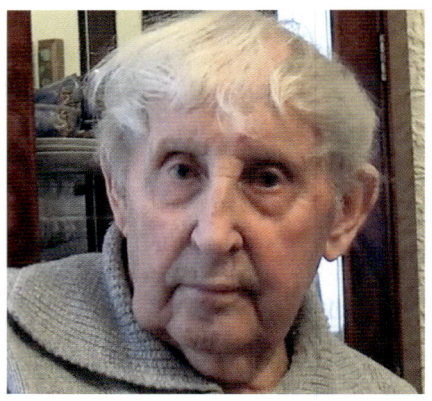

Charlie Barnes in Prestatyn, 2012.

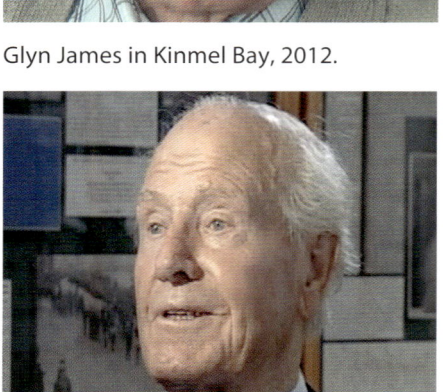

Airman George Duffee, who evaded capture and escaped over the Pyrenees into Spain.

Wyndham Scourfield in Narberth, 2010.

Oliver Lindsay, who was 17 when his boat was torpedoed and sunk on an Arctic convoy.

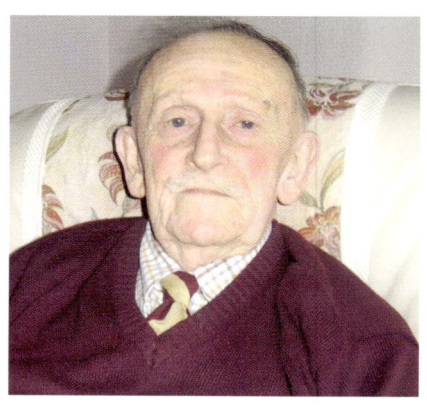

Stewart Johnson in Prestatyn, 2012.

Sgt Major Les Spence of the 77th Heavy Anti-Aircraft Regiment, who kept a secret diary of his captivity on Java and in Japan.

Jem Spence

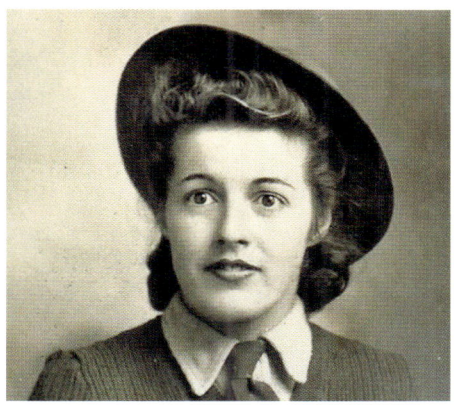

Mary Bott, who learned to farm as a Land Girl to support the war effort.

Mary Bott MBE

Charles Ackerman, who faced execution by a German officer – until another German stepped in and saved his life.

Charles Ackerman

Richard Pelzer, who took part in a top-secret operation early in the morning on D-Day.

Richard Pelzer

Air mechanic Ernest Gane captures a kamikaze attack on HMS *Formidable*, 4 May 1945.
Ian Gane, via WWVA

RN Beach Commandos in Bombay, 1945. Archie Thomas front left, Jack Ball front right, both from Neath Port Talbot.
Archie Thomas, via WWVA

Nagasaki after the atom bomb, 1945. From the album of Royal Welch Fusilier Duncan Hilling.

Duncan Hilling, via WWVA

Sgt Hugh Edwards (far left) with survivors from his regiment, at their POW camp after the Japanese surrender.

Revd Hugh Edwards

Royal Welch Fusiliers parading in front of Emperor Hirohito's Palace, Tokyo, 1945.

Duncan Hilling, via WWVA

your guns, boys. For you the war's over." I couldn't believe
it. It was a German tank, a Tiger tank – and he spoke better
English than I did, because I always had a Welsh accent.

After many months in Italian prison camps, Ron found
himself being handed over to the Germans. It was the start
of a journey which would see him eventually transferred to
German-occupied Poland to work in an I G Farben factory in
the complex of camps known to history as Auschwitz.

Hugh Edwards and the sportsmen of the 77th Heavy Anti-
Aircraft Regiment were no longer based around south Wales
with their guns. They were in a convoy headed for the deserts
of the Middle East. But the Japanese attack on Pearl Harbor
on 7 December 1941 changed things, and they were diverted
to the Far East.

Their troopship arrived in Batavia (now Jakarta) on Java
on 3 February 1942. But it was a lost cause. The Japanese
Army was sweeping through the region, and as the Army
ordered the 77th by train to defend the east of the island,
disaster struck.

Another member of the 77th, Les Spence, recorded the
event in his diary:

February 4/5, 1942. We left by train for Surabaya at 6.30 a.m.,
all in wonderful spirit... We stopped at our last station at
11 p.m. and on leaving, we sang 'Cwm Rhondda'. Then
at 3 a.m. in the morning a terrible catastrophe befell us.

A head-on collision with a goods train loaded with bombs
and petrol. It was terrible. I found poor old Ken dead. Some
had terrible injuries and I do not think they will live.

The troop train had crashed into an ammunition train.
Around 30 members of the 77th were killed and nearly 100
injured. The cause of the crash remained unknown, although
some suggest a signalman loyal to the Japanese might have

been responsible. The 'poor old Ken' referred to by Spence was Battery Sergeant Major Ken Street, a well-known rugby forward who had played for Wales.

For several days, the remaining men of the 77th tried to defend Java. But for both British and Dutch forces on the island, the situation was hopeless.

> March 8, 1942. A day that will live in my memory. The Dutch Army surrendered and we were left with the baby. We were ordered to fight on but later the order was countermanded... I never thought I would live to see this day out.

The following day, Spence noted:

> We've surrendered after being on this island for six weeks... So the war is over as far as we are concerned. Just prisoners of war.

How did it feel to be captured? Hugh Edwards said:

> Not very pleasant. We didn't know what the future would be. We wouldn't know how long it was going to be.

Surrender was to be just the start of the 77th's story. For well over three and a half years, they would suffer the hardship and deprivation of life as Far East prisoners of war. Many would never return to Wales.

On 30 January 1944, at 20,000 feet, John Martin (who was born and bred in London but moved to Wales in later life) was on his third raid. The target was Berlin. Back in Little Rissington in the Cotswolds, working as a flight mechanic, was his girlfriend, Adelaide Jarman, whom he had asked out just a few weeks earlier. The Lancaster in which John was the wireless operator was seven miles short of the German capital when...

We got attacked by a night fighter. Berlin was a hot target, and we were coming up to the target when we were hit.

There were cannon shells ripping around my right arm. Blue flashing lights all over. I think that the navigator must have been injured. I knew we had been badly hit and switched on the intercom just in time to hear the skipper say, "Bale out, bale out!" The navigator couldn't have been very badly hit because he and I were both getting our parachutes on at the same time. As I opened the door at the back of the cockpit to go down to our exit position, flames came at me and I saw that the whole of the fuselage was ablaze. In the split second that I opened the door, I saw the mid-upper gunner climbing out of his turret, which was completely wrecked, and I knew that all I could do was to slam the door shut, so I went back into the cockpit.

The aircraft was in a terrific dive. I climbed into the pilot's seat [he was trying to get out through the escape hatch in the nose of the aircraft, which had been blocked by the bomb-aimer's body]. I tried the dingy hatch but that wouldn't move, and just thought to myself, 'Well, that's my lot.'

I then remembered that I hadn't turned off the Identification Friend or Foe button on the wireless set, so I went back to the set and turned the two buttons to switch it off. The next thing I heard was this enormous explosion, and I was knocked unconscious.

I half came to outside of the aircraft, and saw this huge piece of Lancaster sail very closely past me and then my parachute jerked me into consciousness. I don't remember pulling the ripcord at all and what I imagine happened was that the ripcord got tangled up by the wreckage of the aircraft and was snagged by that. So I was extremely lucky. When we had been first attacked, we were at 20,000 feet, but by the time I regained some consciousness, I must have only been around 1,000 feet from the ground. Part of my harness had been ripped off, but I was aware enough to realise that I needed to cling onto the straps as hard as I could until I hit the ground, far harder than I should have done.

I was challenged by these two guards with rifles and bayonets. They took me across the road and into a hut. I am certain now that they were a searchlight unit, and they really looked after me – they were very kind. Had I dropped into Berlin a little further on, it could have been a different story altogether. These were military men and it was the civilians [Berliners] you had to watch out for. You can understand their feelings and why, because our civilians felt the same way about German airmen during the Blitz, when we would be delighted to hear that one had been shot.

They were very considerate, and this medical Sergeant spent quite a long time checking me over for different things and kept probing me to check for shrapnel. I had bad gashes in my legs, which I think had been caused by shrapnel which may have come from the anti-aircraft fire.

They then took me off to their headquarters and I was told to lie on the floor. I thought I had hidden my parachute very well, but they had found it and tossed it to me and told me to lie down on the floor. I was so knocked about that I lay down on it as best I could. The Sergeant sat at the desk during the night, keeping an eye on me. I didn't want to sleep very much since they were not sleeping either.

Then quite early in the morning, they moved me from this room and took me into part of their living quarters. They weren't too hostile and seemed to be very envious of me, telling me that for me the war was over, and I thought to myself that they might like to be in my position.

John watched the next day as a vehicle pulled up.

Our flight engineer, David Alletson, arrived in the back of a terrific Mercedes-Benz. It was a wonderful-looking vehicle, with two very smart Luftwaffe officers. Having already picked up David, they now came to collect me. They put me in the back seat and we were forbidden to talk to each other. The officer in the passenger seat was holding his pistol the whole time to guard against any attempt of us making an escape or anything like that.

We were taken to Tempelhof Aerodrome in the middle of Berlin and put in a cellar, where we met up with several other RAF bomber crews. Most of them looked really knocked about, as we were of course, and I certainly needed some medical attention. I'd had a bad blow to my head and my legs were lacerated.

The day after we arrived at Tempelhof, they did give me some medical attention at a medical centre. In the medical centre, there were all these civilian women there and I wondered what they were doing at an airfield. Years later, I learned that below Tempelhof airfield were masses of underground tunnels where they did nothing else but repair damaged [Focke-Wulf] Fw 190s. The women were working on the Fw 190s and occasionally needed medical attention, so came up for a bit of treatment in the centre. They quickly spotted who I was and turned on me. I was being escorted by a guard who could not have been more than 17 years old and didn't seem to know what he was doing, so I pushed him back against the wall, so I could see what was happening, as they were spitting and snarling at me.

From Tempelhof, John was transferred to the interrogation centre for airmen at Dulag Luft, near Frankfurt am Main.

We were put in an ordinary passenger train and warned by our armed guard to conceal ourselves as much as possible, because the civilian population were being extremely hostile towards Allied airmen. So we kept as quiet as possible. Eventually and without incident, we arrived at Frankfurt rail station.

But there, something happened without warning. A plateman [someone who maintains the track] twigged on to who we were and leapt up from the rail track and onto the platform, and set about us. He took a swipe at one of our members with a hammer or a hatchet or something. I don't think he actually connected, more of a glancing blow as the RAF chap managed to dodge it. But what it did was to catch the attention of the civilian population, that we were there and who we were.

The crowds on the platform started surging towards us, wanting to get their hands on us. But luckily the German Sergeant in charge of the escort party knew his job very well and immediately pushed us against the wall, and with his men formed a semicircle around us. He made it quite clear that he was going to open fire if these civilians came any nearer. Very grudgingly they gradually edged away – shouting, I imagine, all sorts of curses at us.

And then, funnily enough, after arriving at Frankfurt rail station we transferred onto a tram to get to Dulag Luft, which was in the suburbs of Frankfurt. It was a funny way to transport prisoners and we had a tram for ourselves, with a substantial guard. We were delivered quite close to the entrance of the Dulag Luft.

10

D-Day: 6 June 1944

"We were being thrown about a lot because the pilot
was taking evasive action. And then in no time at
all, of course, the red light and then the green, we
dropped through the bottom, through the floor of
the aeroplane, and off we went!"

NICK ARCHDALE

IN THE SPRING of 1944, the British Isles became the focal
point for all the preparations for the invasion of Europe, and
the defeat of Nazi Germany. Whilst most knew the invasion
of Europe was imminent, hardly any serving personnel knew
when or where it would take place.

Advising Eisenhower on the weather conditions for
D-Day was Group Captain James Stagg's small meteorological
team, which included Flying Officer H H McKay. His new
wife, WAAF Corporal Jean McKay, was expecting her
first child. Jean recalled from her home in Aberporth that
having recently been discharged from the WAAF due to her
pregnancy, the couple lived in Broadway, not far from RAF
Honeybourne, where her husband was stationed. The highly
secret nature of her husband's work was to remain largely
unknown, even to her, though her husband was awarded a
Mention in Despatches on 8 June 1944.

Florence Paul of the Women's Royal Navy Service, whose
members were usually known as 'Wrens', had been sent to

HMS *Eaglet*, the Royal Navy base in Liverpool in February 1944. She performed cypher duties in the office of the Commander-in-Chief, Western Approaches, and, although she did not know it at first, the posting was in preparation for the D-Day landings. Her future husband, Tony Bird, remembered:

> We didn't know what was happening for a while. I was stationed on a Flower-class corvette, based at Sheerness. We knew that there was a tremendous build-up of troops on the southern coast, but we had no idea that we were going to invade France. We sailed from Sheerness to Portsmouth and we were held there for two days because of bad weather.

ATS (Auxiliary Territorial Service) plotter Enid Lloyd from Neath was in Chatham from January 1944 through to D-Day, and in her diary for 1944 she recorded the Army creating artificial fog on the River Medway for two weeks prior to the invasion, so that the troops could prepare for the big day without being seen by any German aircraft flying overhead.

Recovering from injuries sustained after a crash with a US Army truck, RASC despatch rider Gordon Prime heard his regiment was being sent to Tilbury Docks.

> I got the medical officer to sign me back on duty because I didn't want to be left behind:
>
> "No way, I'm not leaving my mates."
>
> "OK," he said, but he gave me one of these elasticated things to go on my knee. It was a terrible pain. We got up to Tilbury and arrived at this tented camp, just outside the docks. We got in and it was barbed wire... just like a prisoner of war camp. Anyway, we were in bell tents. About six to eight of us, I suppose, to a tent and on the gate was a military policeman.
>
> "Oh no, you're not going out."

We couldn't go out. We were locked in! Exactly like prisoners of war! And we were there for five days, locked in. We did have a bit of a NAAFI meal every day – mess tin, you know – but they took us down every day to the docks to load the big American Liberty ship.

They took all our trucks, loaded them on board – tanks, guns, and we had Sherman tanks. Three tiers, three decks. They made, like, a deck and put bunks in for us. Down below was all the ammunition, trucks and stuff. On deck, they put in a shelter, and a long wooden trough with water flowing through it. That was a toilet.

On 3 June, Wrens cypher officer Florence Paul boarded HMS *Aristocrat*, which had 25 officers and 55 men quartered on board. These included naval signalmen to direct and control the tugs, blockships and other craft employed in the construction work on Mulberry B – a harbour to be created off the Normandy coast once the invasion was under way.

The Allied leaders believed these temporary harbours would be key to the success of the Allied efforts to move inland after D-Day. They planned Mulberry A for Omaha Beach in the American sector (although it was damaged by a storm soon after the invasion and abandoned) and Mulberry B for Gold Beach. These were to be towed to the coast of Normandy, where they would be installed so that the Allied forces could bring tanks and vehicles ashore in huge numbers.

Richard Pelzer, from Llansamlet, knew a lot about Mulberry B. Having been called up in 1943, Richard had been sent to the Royal Engineers because of his training as a stonemason. He had also already done two years in the Home Guard.

Posted to Scotland and made to sign the Official Secrets Act, he helped to assemble sections of Mulberry B.

The parts were made previously in different fabricating
places around the country, and they were all brought
together and assembled in Scotland. But we had no idea what
it was all going to be used for.

In fact, Richard would get to Normandy well ahead of it, as he
would play an even more secret role on D-Day.

Back in Tilbury Docks, Gordon Prime remembered:

We boarded the ship Sunday morning [4 June]. We'd been
briefed, we'd been paid out in French money, and we
thought, 'Oh, good: this is it,' because we'd been on so many
exercises.

The officers had been briefed over locations. We hadn't.
Sunday morning, people going to church, I always remember
this: "Say a prayer for us." Anyway, we got on and all went
on deck and the officers got this map out and showed us. We
still didn't know it was Normandy, but we were shown a line:
a beach, a massive, long beach, mainly church steeples.

We were heading for Juno Beach.

The Allied leaders had given each of the five D-Day beaches
a codename: Utah, Omaha, Gold, Juno and Sword. All were
defended by the Germans, not only with heavy machine gun
emplacements but also with concrete and steel obstacles
placed across the sand. This is where Royal Engineer Richard
Pelzer's second secret role would come in.

By the summer of 1944 Richard had become a crack diver
and an expert in removing explosive ordnance devices and
booby traps.

On 6 June, before the invasion troops reached the shore,
he and a small number of his colleagues from what was
called 1051 Port Maintenance Company, arrived somewhere
off Arromanches – and the area codenamed Gold Beach – in
a motor torpedo boat.

We left the ship and swam the last couple of hundred yards. This was before the ships started firing, and the Germans didn't know we were coming. We were there to disarm the defences, because all the beaches had these poles and cross irons and God knows what. We had to get rid of them the best we could. We couldn't use any explosives, nothing like that. A couple of boys lost their lives – killed by explosives.

Richard was back on his boat when the invasion started, but he had to continue to move obstacles throughout the day.

But the first major action would take place inland, on a bridge over the Caen Canal at Bénouville, which would become known to history as Pegasus Bridge. Nick Archdale and the 7th (Light Infantry) Parachute Battalion were to be going in shortly after the Oxfordshire and Buckinghamshire Light Infantry, who would take the bridge.

Late on 5 June, they were driven to an aerodrome, where they blackened their faces and loaded onto a Stirling bomber. Nick's CO was Lieutenant Colonel Geoffrey Pine-Coffin, and the Assistant Adjutant was pre-war actor and future major movie star Lieutenant Richard Todd. Nick recalled…

…opening the bomb doors and looking down and seeing the white wave tops in the Channel. Then, as soon as we got over the [French] coast, of course, there was a lot of anti-aircraft fire. I discovered later on that we had a night fighter on our tail as well. We were being thrown about a lot because the pilot was taking evasive action.

And then in no time at all, of course, the red light and then the green, we dropped through the bottom, through the floor of the aeroplane, and off we went!

Nick jumped into the darkness above occupied France at about 1 a.m. But the anti-aircraft fire had a devastating effect on his unit.

Sadly, one of our two [Short] Stirlings was shot down at a place called Douvres-la-Délivrande before all my boys could get out. And they're mostly buried in the churchyard at Douvres-la-Délivrande, about 10 miles from Caen.

Did he realise then that he was involved in something huge?

Oh yes, very much so. And the extraordinary thing was that when you got on the ground, the first thing you thought was, 'Good God, I'm in France!' You know, you could hardly believe it. Or the fact you were not being shot at. Because you didn't know what to expect at all. It was all new to us because, you know, we were all boys really.

Unfortunately, the evasive action taken by their aircraft meant they had not been dropped where intended.

We were meant to get together and run to the bridge from there. But we were all over the place. People were dropped in every direction. And we had been told, "You'll know exactly where to go because the aeroplanes will all be going in the same direction." And, of course, they were all going in every direction! And so you couldn't tell from that.

Then I heard somebody coming along towards me. And of course, I was challenged, and I forgot the password! But I had to say, "Oh, for Christ's sake, it's me!" And I got together with two or three of my boys who were there and we worked out where we were and set off up a path on the east side of the river, up to the river bridge. And things started to happen there.

The 'Ox and Bucks' had successfully taken the bridge just after midnight. Nick Archdale's unit reached them at about 3 a.m. He crossed the bridge and, as many of the radios weren't working, he went around the battalion to liaise with the various units.

And then, you know, reality began to dawn. I had a bullet hit the wall a quarter of an inch from my left eye, as I was trying to peep around a corner. I learnt about fieldcraft very quickly then: you don't stick your head out and look around corners! But it all became real, and it was a very exciting day.

The strange thing was, we were all mixed up: there were German patrols between us and our battalion headquarters, you know, and we were behind their front line and they were behind ours, really. And I think we were quite good at our job and made the best of it. But it was an exciting day. Cowboys and Indians in real life was what it felt like.

Nick and his men were not only out of touch with many of their comrades, they also had no idea how the invasion was progressing.

Then, at a certain time, the huge barrage from the sea started and there was a terrific rumbling sound, like a giant thunderstorm… and so we knew this was prior to the landings on the beaches taking place. We knew that was starting up.

Tony Bird, further back out at sea, remembered:

D-Day approached. We were ordered to pick up a convoy which was heading for Arromanches – but we didn't know that at the time.

My most vivid memory of the invasion was the tremendous number of aircraft flying over, as we were going cross-Channel – there were literally hundreds of aircraft going over, obviously going in to drop their troops inland, in anticipation of the invasion.

Gordon Prime recalled:

Sunday afternoon, we picked our [barrage] balloon up
– every freighter carried a balloon... about 500 foot – and
went down the Thames Estuary. First light, we went through
the Straits of Dover. We could see the French coast, and the
guns at Calais started firing at us, bloody great guns. Luckily,
they missed us by miles, but a massive spout of water went
up. Anyway, we got through that and that evening we got off
the Isle of Wight, thousands and thousands of ships and God
knows. We sailed over that night.

Tony Bird's ship had set off just before dawn.

[We were] escorting hundreds of ships, towing assault craft
and carrying assault craft on their davits [cranelike devices
for suspending equipment], but thousands of troops were
lining the rails and I noticed that a lot of them were seasick
because the sea was quite choppy. I was headed to Sword
Beach, which is just off Arromanches, and as we approached,
very heavy fire came from the Germans and our battleships
were lobbing 15-inch and 18-inch shells inland. Assault craft
were bobbing about in the choppy seas. Sword Beach was
pretty heavily defended, with spikes and barbed wire.

I had a bullet whizz past my left ear, and that's the nearest
I came to being shot on D-Day. But unfortunately the LCAs
[landing craft] were hit by shells, and I'm afraid that the
bodies were floating around in the water and we couldn't
make any effort to recover them, because the main object of
the attack was to get troops on land. Luckily, we succeeded.

Gordon Prime remembered seeing that the RAF had bombed
the beaches and hearing the roar of shells from the Royal Navy
as they flew over his head.

We were still on this Liberty ship; and the rocket-firing ships,
as well, were bashing them on the beaches... 07:30 was

H-Hour [the time at which the operation commenced] for the British, and we were about 09:30 by that time.

The weather was pretty rough. I think it was a four- or six-foot swell, and these landing craft came alongside. It wasn't a British landing craft, it was American LCT – Landing Craft, Tank – much smaller than the British. It was bobbing like a cork. We went down these rope ladders after they'd loaded all our stuff onto the landing craft. You had to wait for the thing to come up and jump, otherwise you missed it!

In the meantime, while they were unloading, I was on deck. I didn't know what was going on and I heard this 'bang' and I thought, 'Oh, God, we've been hit.' What had happened was, the Sherman tank when loading had been no problem as they used dockside cranes, but to unload they had to use these horrible derricks, thin derricks that freighters had. They got this Sherman, just going to go over the side… it went straight to the bottom, 'bang'. The derrick had broken, and this American sailor, he said if they hadn't put seven foot of earth at the bottom as ballast, it would have gone straight through the bottom. It went all through the planking, anyway… The next thing, one of our three-tonners, the same thing happened, but that dropped on top of a landing craft. They chucked it over the side, carried on. Anyway, we eventually started going ashore.

On one of the landing craft approaching the nearest beach was Ted Owens. Ted crossed the Channel early on the morning of 6 June with his unit, 41 Commando.

We'd been 48 hours on the boat because the invasion had been postponed and the weather was very, very bad. And those type of boats were flat bottomed, so you'd get seasick very easily. But – big-head – I didn't get seasick and I was showing off to the men. Then it came over on the tannoy to get some food into you because you didn't know when you were going to have your next meal. So I picked up a tin of oxtail soup and they were self-heating: you'd strike them on the top and heat would go down through them, and they were nice and hot to drink. I drank that and within about five or seven minutes, I was like the rest: I was lying on the floor. Oh, I was seasick. And I've never eaten oxtail since then. I can't stand the smell of it.

And, of course, then, when we could hear the gunfire, the heavy ships on the outside of us were firing away, and you could hear the shells going over your head. It's the weirdest sound you ever heard. It was like a 'we-we-we-we-we' as it was going over, and that's the big shells. And then you had a lot of planes flying over and a lot of other boats there as well, destroyers and stuff: they were firing their guns.

Then, when we got in close, and I walked down that gangway onto the beach, I could see the bodies there, and I heard a voice shouting, "Concentrate your fire on the building in front of you." Well, they had the tanks lining up there and all the men would hide behind the tanks. This tank on the left was knocked out and I ran to that, put my rifle over the tracks of the rear end of the tank, and I put, oh, I don't know, four, five, six rounds into the aperture on the building. It looked like real windows but they weren't: there was just slits and the guns coming out. But I guarantee I put my five or six rounds in there. I mean, it was only 200 yards – you couldn't miss.

But Ted's luck quickly ran out.

A shell came over and hit the turret of the tank and the shrapnel, just like an umbrella, came down over the top of me. I felt the pain when the metal hit me, because that's white hot when it hits you. It went into my shoulder and my back. I didn't go unconscious, or anything like that, but I was completely flat on my face. I could hear what was going on around me, but I could not move. I couldn't move one finger. I was absolutely paralysed.

There was a last-minute change of plan for Idwal Symonds and 46 Commando, who left the Solent on a Belgian ship named after the Swedish-born Queen of Belgium.

> Before the war our landing ship, the *Prinses Astride*, was a Belgian Railways cross-Channel ship running from Ostend to Harwich, and she had been converted into a Commandos' assault ship.

Despite months of training for a cliff assault, the Commandos were told there was to be a last-minute change of plan.

> The cliff assault was cancelled on the morning of D-Day when we were going to go in, and we were redirected to the beach. The beach landing was quite easy, really. A certain amount of firing, but they should all be firing high; the bullets were all over my head. But we did lose a few men during that assault.
>
> The beach had a seawall of about 10 feet high, and on top of that seawall was a road running parallel with the sea, and leading to Caen. We came up to the seawall and it was not feasible to climb it – it was concrete. So we went to the west, towards the mouth of a small river, and we got off the beach onto the road.
>
> But at the far end of that road was a large house – it looked like a small hotel – and it was full of Germans. We attacked that. And they all surrendered. They looked very, very pleased to surrender. I'll never forget how grateful they looked. In fact, some of them had little parcels ready with their personal things in!

The cliff assault troops of 46 Commando had learnt their objective. Idwal remembered:

To the east of the landing beaches were two rivers running parallel, the Orne and the Oise, and on the other side of the rivers were steep cliffs. The cliffs were a hard clay rather than rock – just like those we'd trained on, on the Isle of Wight – and on top of those cliffs was a German gun battery. And that was our objective.

Charlie Barnes was an anti-aircraft gunner on LST 322: a Landing Ship, Tank, which was specifically built to land vehicles on beaches.

All the ships were in a line and they were firing into Caen. All you could hear was the gunfire. The noise was terrible. Terrible. You couldn't hear yourself talk.

Our first landing was all their vehicles, you know, and then the second one was the same, and then the third one was troops, full of troops. The worst thing of the landing was, when you dropped the lads off, you had to wait for the tide to come in again to take you out again. That was the biggest problem. It was terrible.

When we got up to the beach, the troops just ran ashore. Drop them off and wait for the tide and then we went out again, back to Portsmouth, got another load and come back and there were wrecks all over the beaches. We came back about three or four times. That's all you want to go and all!

I was an AA [anti-aircraft] gunner and we had our own barrage balloon, but we got attacked by aircraft. It was murder. But by the fourth trip everything had gone on inland.

Tony Bird remembered…

…thousands of assault craft going in, bodies floating in the water, shells coming over, aircraft coming over to drop parachutists inland. It was a feat of arms which had never been surpassed and never will be again. And I salute all these Army people who actually landed, who actually fought hand-to-hand in France, because in the Navy we were a little remote. We were on the sea, a little divorced from the land, so we don't actually see what's going on.

Ted Owens lay on the sand codenamed Sword Beach as his comrades moved onto the dry land. The shrapnel which had showered down onto him had left him paralysed but conscious.

> After a while – it could have been about 10 minutes or could have been an hour, I don't know – I heard voices come up and one of them said, "This poor blighter has had it." And they turned me over and my eyes moved. And he said, "Oh no, he's alive. His eyes moved."

The two medics stuck a label on Ted, noting what wounds he had, and then he was lifted onto a stretcher.

> They took me down onto a landing craft. There were loads of other wounded there, and a couple of Germans. And they took me to a Canadian hospital ship, floating off. And they put us on a derrick and lifted us onboard. And then they gave me a new thing out, an injection – they called it a 'twilight sleep'. And then I didn't know where I was.

Going onto Juno Beach, Gordon Prime recalled:

> I can remember, there were two Sherman trucks in front of me. I was driving a truck then. All our trucks were loaded with supplies – not fully loaded because of the getting up the beaches. The one I drove was three-ton weight of high explosive shells, 200 gallons of petrol in jerry cans and my motorcycle on the back of that. The Sergeant Major said, "You're not riding them down the ramp, you're driving a truck."

We'd been briefed: "When you get onto the beach, look in the dunes and there'll be big markers about six, eight foot square."

The beach group had set these big screens up and a white cross. If you were driving a vehicle that was your exit. They'd cleared the mines, the Royal Engineers. We went through the gap and we just bashed on inland, for about half a mile, I suppose.

Anyway, we got to this village and we pulled in this field and of course, the first thing you do is dig in, dig a slit trench, get down below. So we dug in. There were these French refugees, walking with horses and carts, and families on the move and whatnot, little kids with them, passing us. We were on 24-hour ration packs, which consisted of dehydrated tea and all sorts. We had a bar of chocolate – Nestlé's plain chocolate – and I didn't like plain chocolate. We had a load of these and I remember giving these little French kids this chocolate – who hadn't seen chocolate for years, I suppose. Anyway, we sorted ourselves out and we spent the night there, where we were dug in.

During the night there was quite a bit of activity. They used to come over mainly at night, the German aircraft. Every bloomin' civilian freighter had Oerlikon guns. They'd be firing them up there, and their tracers were going everywhere. But the trouble was, every ship had its own [barrage] balloon and of course all these balloons were filled with hydrogen. They hit one. In the end, Montgomery issued an order that the only people to use ack-ack [anti-aircraft] guns were the gunners themselves.

Our company motto was 'Bash on regardless', and that's just what we did. Our assembly area now was a little village called Tailleville, which was one mile inland from Juno Beach, from the little town Saint-Aubin-sur-Mer. "Here's the map reference, jump on your bike and go and find this field." And I had to take the coast road all the way up.

The field I was heading for was on the other side of the village. There was a little duck pond on the right and a driveway, and there was a gateway and that was the one, so I thought, 'This is it.' So then I had to go all the way back and lead the B platoon, as it was then, to this field and we set our headquarters up in this field.

Anyway, we all moved in and we set our headquarters up just inside the gate, dug in. And, of course, the first thing you do, as well, when you stop, is for all the vehicles to be scrimmed-up with camouflage netting. You weren't allowed to walk across the field: you had to stick to all round the edge – drive round, walk, because a [German] reconnaissance aircraft could even pick up a footprint. All the trucks moved in and as I was messing about motorcycling, I was the last to dig a hole, dig my slit trench. The boys had all dug in nicely and I thought, 'Where the hell am I going to put my trench now?' And I moved across the field – the only place was a dead German's grave. They'd buried him the day before and I had to dig my slit trench about three foot away from him. His rifle stuck in the ground with his helmet on top and I thought, 'Oh', and I lay there at night thinking, 'He is three foot away...' Anyway, I wasn't squeamish, luckily.

Idwal Symonds's unit followed the river inland to the town of Douvres-la-Délivrande, then known simply as Douvres.

When we got to Douvres, the German resistance hardened considerably and fighting became quite intense. We had quite a lot of casualties. I fortunately wasn't hit at all. And I didn't take cover, I stood up most of the time. I was resigned to the possibility of not surviving those few days, so I had no problem staying on my feet. And that's where we stayed for a little while, while the build-up on the beaches went on. But we were one of the first to land on D-Day. And we did what we had to do. We were successful.

Nick Archdale's platoon in the 7th (Light Infantry) Parachute Battalion had defended the Caen road outside Bénouville for most of 6 June. They were then withdrawn and told to sleep in someone's garden.

> I now had the remains of A company, which was 11 men only. 11 from 120. The rest were injured or killed. Some never managed to get back to us. Quite a lot kept on coming in in odd lots during the day and the next day.
>
> Speaking of my platoon: I'd had four Sergeants [a platoon Sergeant and one to each section] when we landed and by the evening of the first day, I had one Sergeant left – three of them had been killed. That was the sad and awful part.

The following morning, Nick and what was left of his platoon were ordered to take up a position looking towards Bréville, up the hill from Ranville.

> I was looking across this large wheat field with my field glasses, when I suddenly realised that there were a whole lot of German troops coming across the field, spread out. And so we waited a bit and let them get reasonably close and then started dropping two-inch mortar bombs behind them. And, poor devils, I think they must have had a horrible time because as they got up and ran, we were shooting them. And I always remember my commanding officer, Lieutenant Colonel Pine-Coffin, arriving to see what was going on and insisting on taking a rifle and having a shot himself.

After D-Day, Richard Pelzer stayed in France and "worked up the coast, clearing all the harbours so that we could get supplies in":

> We were checking that the Germans hadn't booby-trapped the lock gates, and things like that. Checking that they

weren't sabotaged, because the Germans were retreating and could leave a surprise.

We did Courseulles, Deauville, Trouville – right up the coast. Any little inlet we were in.

The next biggest job was to get Boulogne operative. The Germans had put explosives in the quayside by every crane in one of the docks. And when [British soldiers] put the electric on in the docks – when they had that operating again – all the cranes on one quayside fell into the dock.

Then we did Calais. The Calais job was to prepare the dock and repair the slipway for the trains to be disembarked.

Despite his D-Day injuries, Ted Owens spent only ten weeks out of the front line, mainly at the Miners' Hospital in Caerphilly.

When I was in hospital, I had to lie on my right side, because my left shoulder and shoulder blade were badly injured, and I had such a big hole in my shoulder. They had a 10-inch bandage and that was all soaked in penicillin, and they'd fold that, push it into the hole. They changed that bandage once every four days and that was absolutely excruciating; you thought your toenails and everything were coming with it. But I have always had great respect for that hospital. I would love to go back to it and give a nice big bunch of flowers.

His treatment complete, Ted was given four or five days to spend with his family before being sent back to Normandy.

I joined my unit at a place called Pont L'Évêque. Soon after I got there, there was a massive explosion: the Germans blew up their own ammunition dump before they retreated.

There was quite a heavy fight there with a very large concrete bunker, and there was a Polish regiment there and they fired half a dozen of these big blockbuster bombs – petards – which were about the size of a dustbin. When they hit that place, they just literally buried it. And I think that was a terrible thing to hear those men down inside of it. That shook me up.

And I saw something there… I had a special friend, a Corporal. And he was the gentlest boy you ever met. A very, very gentle man. And he did something very nasty and I was a bit annoyed about it. These Germans were in the bunker and he threw a phosphorus grenade down there, and I said, "Oh, that's a terrible thing to do," and a few swear words. And he came up to me – and no man would have done it normally – and he just poked me in the chest. "Taffy," he said. "You can shut your mouth. You don't know what's going on. You've just come back from Blighty. You've seen nothing." He'd been there all the way from D-Day. I was lost for words. I couldn't believe how he'd changed. Apparently, some of the men from the Commando unit had been shot in the back of the head and he'd seen it. And he was very unforgiving after that.

11

Maquis and Escape Lines

"The men must have been informed on, for one morning,
about 4 a.m., a lorry-load of Germans arrived in the
village and stopped on the green right outside our house.
They then ran to the house being occupied by the Armée
Blanche men and broke the door down."

JOHN EVANS

PEMBROKESHIRE BOMBER PILOT John Evans had been shot
down over Belgium in March 1944. Stuck in a wooded area,
he wondered what to do next and began to move through the
trees. He was walking with one boot; the other having been
wrenched off during his parachute jump to safety.

Obviously, what you have to do is find someone to help you.
So with this in mind, I moved around, and I suddenly heard
some singing, like a good Welsh male voice choir. I walked
towards where the sound was coming from and I eventually
came to a small road. I peeped out and there was this squad
of German soldiers coming along, singing at the top of their
voices, so I dashed back into the bushes until they had gone.

When they had passed, I went out again. I was walking
down the road and there was this man coming towards me
on a bicycle. He looked like a farm worker of some sort. I
jumped out in front of him. I must have looked dishevelled
with just one boot and so on. He looked more scared than

I was, I think. I tried to explain to him who I was. But he wanted nothing to do with it and he rode off. I had only gone about 20 yards, and he shouted to me and he pointed in the direction I was going and he said, *"Boche, Boche!"* – Germans – and then he pointed to the right, where there was a path, so I went down there and eventually came to a little farmhouse.

I thought, 'I must try something, so I will try here.' I kept an eye open for about half an hour before venturing in, then I went and knocked on the door and a lady opened it. Of course, she was obviously Flemish; she could not speak English, not even French. She knew obviously who I was, I think, but she asked me to come in, and then went to fetch her husband. There were about six or seven small children round the table having a meal of some sort. She asked me to sit down, and he came in. I tried to explain to him again who I was, and he managed to tell me that he would go and fetch some men to help me. In the meantime, I was taken to a barn to have a sleep in the hay up on top of the barn.

John Evans had done what all evading airmen had to do if they wanted a chance to stay free: he had taken a risk and knocked on a door. It was a nervous wait to find out if the people he had put his faith in were really able to help him or if they were so afraid of – or even loyal to – the Germans that they were actually going to turn him in.

But John had been lucky. He was reunited with two of his crew and they went through a series of safe houses and an underground shelter in a forest before a man named Florent Biernaux arrived with bicycles for them. His family ran a section of an underground evasion line in the town of Hasselt.

He could speak quite good English and he told us we would be going to Hasselt to his house on the bikes. So off we went to Hasselt on the main road now. We were spread out, of course, not to cause any suspicion. On the main road we had a bit of a fright. Coming towards us was a German motorcycle and sidecar. They went past us and all of a sudden screeched to a stop and turned the other way, passed us again and I thought, 'Crikey, this is it now,' and then they stopped again. As we drew level, we could see there was something wrong with the bike: they were both down having a look at the bike's engine. We just pedalled away and eventually got to Monsieur Biernaux's house in Hasselt.

From the shelter of the Biernaux back garden, John was able to watch American aircraft attack the bridge on the canal. He was then moved on to Liège and the home of a widow named Louise Delchef. Despite having the appearance of a quiet elderly lady, Madame Delchef hated the occupiers and planned to take part in an uprising against them.

> Her dearest possessions were a couple of machine guns and a number of revolvers with plenty of ammunition, which she kept under the tiles on her roof.

On the morning of 6 June 1944, John and the other evaders in the Delchef home were lying in bed when she came rushing upstairs, the words tumbling out of her mouth about the landing at Normandy.

> She was crying for joy and flung her arms around each of us in turn. We were hardly less excited and immediately rushed out of bed, ran downstairs and switched the radio to the BBC. Sure enough, the great day had arrived. We felt very happy indeed and were convinced that our day of liberation was not far off.
>
> But we had to wait two and a half more long months.

From the home of Madame Delchef in Liège, John and other airmen were moved to a new safe house in the Ardennes: the home of a couple named Vincent and Marie-Ghislaine Wuyts-Denis. Life there was quiet: walks in the woods, bathing in the river, and playing bridge in the afternoon. There didn't seem to be any German troops for miles.

But then, at the end of July, the Germans launched a massive raid on the village. The target was a house on the other side of the church, where four members of the resistance group, the Armée Blanche, were hiding.

The men must have been informed on, for one morning, about 4 a.m., a lorry-load of Germans arrived in the village and stopped on the green right outside our house. They then ran to the house being occupied by the Armée Blanche men and broke the door down.

One of the men fired at the German officer and wounded him, and he and another were promptly mown down by a machine gun.

A third was running away through the fields behind the house when he was shot. The fourth was hiding in a cellar beneath the house and the Germans did not find him.

After they had killed all the occupants, as they thought, the soldiers burned the house down and went away. But before they left, the officer warned the Burgomaster that if any more recalcitrants were found, then the whole village would be burned to the ground.

When the Germans arrived, Vincent and Ghislaine shook the airmen awake and pushed them quickly out through the back door, pointing them to the nearby woods.

There was clearly a state of some panic, but it was obvious that the Germans did not know of our presence as they made no attempt to enter our house. It was also clear that the person who had denounced the young men would have done the same for us had he been aware of our existence there.

After the raid, it was deemed too dangerous to return to the house and John and the others remained in the woods for four days and nights before a new safe house could be found.

John's last weeks on the run were spent in a series of large forest camps, holding several dozen airmen. Food was scarce, but there was a great sense that the war had turned against the Germans.

> There was a road not too far away and we could hear the rumble of German vehicles as they retreated along it. Occasionally, Allied fighter planes would appear and attack the retreating convoys and when this occurred, the Germans would scatter into the woods alongside the road – but never far enough to encounter us.
>
> Some of the German transport was horse-drawn, and quite often during these attacks horses were killed and were then left on the roadside. This proved to be a welcome source of additional food for the villagers, and for us too. They would come out at night and cut off as much meat as possible, and some of it was brought to the camp, where it was soon cooked and eaten, providing a very acceptable supplement to our meagre rations.

Then a villager arrived to tell the camp the Germans had gone.

> We hurriedly gathered our few belongings and ran down to the village. Every house had a British or American flag flying from the window and the people were beside themselves with joy and welcomed us with open arms.
>
> The main bridge across the Samois had been blown up by the retreating Germans. When we reached it, an American armoured vehicle could be seen on the opposite side of the river.
>
> Our joy was overwhelming. We waved and shouted at the soldiers, took off our shoes and socks and rolled up our trousers, and waded across. The occupants of the American

vehicle could hardly believe their eyes and ears when our unkempt mob approached them, speaking English.

John was transported back to Paris and then to England, where through a series of phone calls a message reached the police station in Goodwick, Pembrokeshire. It was then that after more than three months, John's parents were finally told that their son was alive and well, and would soon be home.

George Duffee spent about the same time on the run as John Evans – and also got home safely.

It took me a total of four months to go from Holland, Belgium, France, over the Pyrenees, eventually to Gibraltar via Seville and Cadiz, and then home. And then we got home in a Dakota – we had to fly way out into the Atlantic to avoid the fighter defences of the Germans, because they used to base them along the coast. And eventually you get back and you're debriefed and they say, "What would you like to do now?" Well, there was a question! I said, "I would like to get back to the squadron." So I did return to the squadron. I completed my tour of 39 operations, and they very kindly gave me a DFC [Distinguished Flying Cross].

Evaders like John and George never forgot their debt to the people who helped them. George said:

They were ordinary people, but extraordinary in their behaviour. It's very difficult to appreciate, but resistance is something you hang on to if someone tries to take freedom away from you. They knew that if they were apprehended by the enemy, they would go to concentration camps or, in some cases, they would be shot. So they took a big risk. I cannot emphasise too much the dedication and valour of these helpers. They were splendid people.

12

Market Garden

"So we got into the woods, well into the woods.
I looked to my left and there were some Germans
coming out, so I fired. Talk about bloody John Wayne!"
CHARLES ACKERMAN

STEWART JOHNSON OF 2nd/5th Battalion Lancashire Fusiliers broke out of Normandy late in August 1944. Recalling the events years later at his home in Prestatyn, he stated:

> We crossed the Seine on a Bailey bridge and then had skirmishes through Belgium. And then we crossed the Wilhelmina Canal and into Holland.

By now, Stewart's unit was attached to the 2nd Battalion, Gordon Highlanders.

> We didn't know anything about the big picture. Most of the time we were only concerned with and knew what was going on in the field next to us or the road just there... And, in fact, even maps were virtually out of date by the time we got them, because the advance got pretty rapid once we were out of Normandy, so we very rarely had maps up to date.

On 17 September, the Allies launched Operation Market Garden, using land and airborne forces to cross the Lower

Rhine and swing east into Germany. Stewart's platoon was among the forces which had to push north up the Dutch roads to meet up with paratroopers seizing the river bridges ahead.

> We saw the airborne people overhead being dropped. It was quite a spectacle. We were looking at them from our slit trenches. It was an Armada in the air. And we thought at the time that all we had to do was to walk through the airborne folk. But it didn't work out like that, as you know!

Stewart's platoon had to help clear the road for the troops and armoured vehicles of XXX Corps to get to Arnhem.

> We were just north of Eindhoven when we found the Germans dug in, 300 yards from the road. We had a company attack and it was a case really of "Fix bayonets and follow me!", but we had no mortar or artillery support.
>
> We went in at dawn, but I didn't get very far. I had gunshot wounds, chest and shoulder, and I fell, fortunately, into a German trench. Several of my platoon were shot down as well. I drifted in and out of consciousness. But the stretcher bearers didn't get to us till evening. But by then, on the radio, I think – probably from Brigade – they must have got through to the RAF. And these rocket-firing [Hawker] Typhoons came in and they cleared the wood. Those rockets were like express trains coming out of the sky. And they were very close.

Carried out by stretcher bearers, Stewart was operated on in a field dressing station before eventually being evacuated to hospital in Brussels.

Charles Ackerman of Cardiff also took part in Market Garden on the 17th. His unit, 4th Battalion, Welch Regiment, had a similar job to Stewart: keep the road open for XXX Corps. But they came up against the same problem.

We came across this wooded area on the left-hand side, which we called Spandau Woods afterwards. And these [German] SP guns [self-propelled artillery] opened up and knocked out three tanks. Well, of course, it blocked the road, so we came to a bloody standstill.

Charles' section was sent to knock the guns out. They had no support: just their rifles and grenades.

So we got into the woods, well into the woods. I looked to my left and there were some Germans coming out, so I fired. Talk about bloody John Wayne! I always had one up the breech, see, so I let go with that, but I never had time to put another one in. Somebody shouted "Grenade!" and one landed just a few feet away. All I could do was turn my back on it. It blew me forward, caught me right across the legs.

All hell let loose. But our boys managed to beat the Germans back a bit. And they advanced further into the woods, a lot of fighting going on. But I was lying in the wood where I fell. I managed to get behind some brambles or something. And I had the sense to wiggle my toes, because all sorts of things were going through my mind, but at least I could wiggle my toes.

But when the Germans counter-attacked through the wood, Charles was terrifyingly exposed.

This one German officer came up to me and he unbuckled his bloody revolver – he had a Mauser. I thought, 'Surely, he's not going to finish us off?' And another soldier, a medic, he put himself between me and the officer – and I swear blind, that German soldier saved my life.

It was a moment which still brought a lump to his throat when he spoke about it decades later at his home in Canton.

Syd Daw and the 52nd (Lowland) Infantry Division had crossed into Belgium and were moving into the Netherlands. Syd was in the sniper section.

The first time I saw real action was in Ghent. And then Holland, especially Middelburg, on Walcheren. They reckon that was the worst battle since D-Day, because we lost so many troops: British, Canadian and Polish – I think thirty-odd thousand in a few days, you know. Nasty conditions, but there we are.

Syd's friends had warned him that snipers were a target. But he enjoyed the freedom he got in the sniper section.

You were left to your own devices, you know. You're on the flank, more often than not, to do things your way. And then I often spent time as a security guard to the Commander. He likes to have one sniper around him to make sure he's safe and sound. But you're left to your own devices. I didn't like being outside tanks, because you can't hear what's going on. You can't hear bullets and things coming towards you. So, yes, it's much better being out of the way – a big advantage.

There was one occasion when I had the longest time without sleep in my life – the best part of 48 hours. My eyes were popping out of my head. This was on the south island, South Beveland, before Walcheren. So the Sergeant says, "Right, you eight, you get your heads down. Don't worry about anything. You'll be safe." We went into this big barn and there was a big pile of straw there. I thought, 'That'll do me.' I picked it up to make a bed, and under the straw was a big dead German. Big, big moustache. Bloated up, you know. But I was so tired, I just dropped onto that and off I went. Had my sleep – a couple of hours, I suppose.

I was used to seeing dead bodies by then. Even my own mates, you know, because people are prepared to die for you, aren't they? You're prepared to die for each other. But when you see your own friends, and you've got to pick them up and throw their body onto the back of a lorry, well, it's not the nicest thing to want to do, is it? But there we are.

During another rest from the front, Syd was taken well behind the lines.

We dug a big trench, two of us, and covered it up with old bits of wood and whatever. We thought, 'We'll have a nice sleep here tonight.' Anyway, there were some airbursts going off. They're not very nice. Instead of hitting the ground and exploding, they explode in the air and the shrapnel comes down, especially in trees and things, killing people. I thought, 'They're coming a bit near now…' Next thing, one exploded and I heard a loud bang – seemed to be the largest bang in my life – and something hit my helmet: bang! Whether it knocked me down, I don't know. This piece of shrapnel that size [a very large nail] was stuck in my helmet. So if I hadn't had a helmet on, I'd have been gone, wouldn't I?

So I said to the Sergeant Major, "I'd rather get back in the line, I know where I am there," you know. "Get in the trench!" he said. But there we are. One of those things. Good fortune, I suppose. Perhaps I said my prayers properly. I think I did. I said quite a few in those days!

Later, Syd saw a German soldier who had not been so lucky.

I went over a dyke and there was a trench there. I walked towards it and I looked in and he's sat there, this young German – only my age, obviously – sat up. And I'm looking at him, and he's got his helmet off, on his lap, and his soft hat on and a bit of shrapnel in his head. Dead, obviously dead. So I just dragged his bag from behind him, saw some pictures that he'd had… with family. Anyway… I took his rifle, took it out and his medal, put it on the side, just covered him up, if you like, so they'd come along and give him a proper burial.

Yes, had he done what I had – left my helmet on – he'd have been alive today, no doubt. Sad. Yes, there's some sad occasions like that, aren't there? Stories to tell, I suppose.

Syd moved onto the island of Walcheren from the south. Ted Owens would arrive as an assault troop, just like on D-Day.

In September 1944, the Allies had taken the port of Antwerp from the Germans. But they couldn't use the port because of the German guns on the coast of Walcheren on the Scheldt Estuary. The island had to be captured too.

Ahead of the assault, the RAF bombed the dykes around the low-lying land of Walcheren and flooded the countryside. This flooded some of the German bunkers and cut off roads.

Ted landed at the town of Westkapelle on 1 November 1944. Up on the dyke, he and his friends fought their way north towards the next town, Domburg.

Oh, it was very hard, very hard going. We got halfway – well, we could see the outskirts of Domburg – and the Germans had laid a lot of mines. And this mine went off with the two boys in front of me. Killed them both.

So we all hit the deck. I was lying there and I was looking forward and I could see some movement. Germans, of course. I shouted back, "Movement ahead of us, Corporal!" "Where?" he said. So I looked up again and there was a big tower there, a church tower. I put my hand up in front of my face and I said, "Three fingers to the right of the tower and two fingers to the left of the windmill." And he lifted his binoculars. "I got them," he said, and he sent a message back and the other troop behind us, Y Troop, they were a mortar team as well. And they gave the Germans a hell of a stonking.

And then the following morning, when we were going to move forward, I said, "There's something wrong with my leg. I can't move." My leg was swollen. I thought I'd hurt it when I dived down onto the ground but when I looked, I could see a hole in my trousers. So I was sent back to the CRS – the Casualty Reception Station – so I limped back and went back to Flushing [Vlissingen] to the CRS, which was in a school and it was all wooden parquet flooring. I said, "I got something wrong with my knee." I still didn't know what it was.

And he got a scalpel out and split the seam of my trousers so he could get them above my knee. He said, "There's a lot of muck here, and pieces of scab. I'll have to get that off." And he started scraping it and then a ball bearing dropped onto the floor, and that's when I knew what it was. A ball bearing from the mine had smacked me in the kneecap. The round hole is still visible there now. And I had that ball bearing in my pocket for a very long time. I was very lucky there.

Ted Owens' action came to an end shortly before Christmas of 1944.

We were in a village on the River Maas. It was somewhere near s'-Hertogenbosch. And we were clearing the houses and there were quite a few snipers there. I was lying on the pavement, looking round a corner, and this shell came over and hit the side of the wall and a piece of metal came down and it went right through my windpipe. And of course, that was about the end of the war for me. I was in hospital then for a while – walking wounded. I was all right. Only my throat was very badly swollen and they had to feed me through a straw. But I spent Christmas 1944 in a Canadian hospital.

Ted's unit, 41 Commando, made its way on into Germany without him.

13

Behind the Wire in
Europe and the Far East

"On more or less the day I was taken prisoner, a
very pompous SS officer came up and said, 'On the
instruction of my Führer, Adolf Hitler, I have to tell you
that you are to be shot because you are Commando.'"

IDWAL SYMONDS

THE WELSHMEN OF the 77th Heavy Anti-Aircraft Regiment
had all been captured in March 1942 by the advancing
Japanese. For the first 18 months, they were kept in two
prison camps on Java. Les Spence from Cardiff kept a daily
account of how they coped with their new life and with the
ever-present fear of death from starvation or disease. He
noted on 28 May 1942:

> Another death occurred today. It's very, very serious, this
> dysentery. I think we are in for a very rough time and many
> good people will die with this disease. I pray to God that I
> will come out safely.

Despite the fear of illness, to keep their spirits up, the men in
the camp quickly got round to organising rugby 'Internationals'
and a football 'league'.

July 2, 1942. Played soccer for the camp and beat number 3 camp 4-0. I did not enjoy the game. I lost my gold identity disc. Am feeling very despondent. I do hope I will find it.

Also playing these games behind the wire fence in Java were Wales International Ernie Curtis, who had been the youngest member of Cardiff City's 1927 FA Cup-winning side; former Cardiff City and Wales forward Billy James; and Cardiff City goalkeeper John 'Jackie' Pritchard. Perhaps the most dominant player, according to the diaries, was Lieutenant Wilfred Wooller, one of Wales' greatest ever all-round sportsmen, proficient at rugby, cricket, football and squash.

Other prisoners turned to religion. Hugh Edwards had been an itinerant preacher before the war and became the camp padre. He and other POWs built a small church at their camp. He remembered:

The service was, shall I say, non-denominational. Couldn't do anything else. And they had to be very simple. We didn't have any hymn books, until the boys got together and decided a particular hymn, 'Abide With Me', or some of the others, and then they'd sit down with a bit of paper and write out the words. People are so used to using a hymn book that they can't sing without one. They'd know the first verse and they'd know the last verse but anything in between, well, they got mixed up.

Everything depended on staying lucky – not catching disease – and on staying as positive as one could. Hugh Edwards recalled:

A lot of it was to do with attitude, and we began to learn other chaps' attitudes and sometimes when they were very miserable, very down, they'd get a thump because that was the only way of telling them that we're noting it as well. But

I've had chaps die next to me because they gave up, and that was a very difficult thing to fight. Hard to believe, isn't it?

Life was tough on Java: food was scarce and the prisoners were made to work to repair a local airfield. But things were to get worse. The occupier needed prisoners to work in Japan and many of the 77th were chosen for the journey. In September 1943 those selected were loaded into the hold of a ship called the *Ussuri Maru*. Conditions on vessels such as this were so uncomfortable that they became known as 'hell ships'. Hugh Edwards said:

> It was five weeks in the hold of a ship. And it's not very funny when you hear big bangs going on outside and other boats are being torpedoed – by Americans. And to hear the water slapping up against the side of the ship. Terrifying, it is, terrifying. I wouldn't like anybody else to go through it. You don't know what to expect. You don't know what's really happening. It's very, very frightening, plays havoc with the nerves and we had five weeks of that. We were allowed up on deck only to go to the toilet.

For the next two years, 'Camp 8 Kamo', near the village of Inatsuki (or Inatsuki-machi) in Kyūshū, southern Japan, would be their home. Stanley Roberts of Barry remembered the huts there were...

> ...the low, weatherboarded type, with felted roofs and raised floors of *tatami* straw matting... Partitions divided the huts into separate rooms, housing four, six or eight men, depending on size, and each was lit by a single light bulb.

This was a coal-mining camp, producing fuel for the Japanese war machine. The prisoners were forced to work in the mine. Hugh Edwards remembered:

The countryside was a bit hilly and mountainous, like we are here in Wales. But the entrance to the coalmine was in the side of the hills and to go in the mine you went in on this sort of a railway affair and it went sloping down. It would stop at various levels until we were somewhere down the bottom… Then we got out of the train and started to walk along the line – I would say probably about half a mile, if not more.

Shifts were usually 10 hours long. But it would take an hour to get there and an hour to get back, so we would be out of the camp about 12 hours. And we would do that for 15 days in the month.

It was very wet and very dark. We had our head lamps, which we had to collect on our way down – but they had an acid battery, which we had to have on our backs, and if these things were leaking, you could get a burn, believe me. But they were the only lights that we had.

The Japanese would work on the [coal] faces. Sometimes we would help to drill the holes about a yard or metre-worth into the face and then they would put in explosive and we would have to come back when they'd blown the faces out. Then we'd have to go in and gather it all up. We were given a basket, an open-ended basket, for carrying and a short-handled tool with a flat blade to scrape at the coal. You'd scrape it and then carry it to the [rail] trucks. And our duty was to fill those trucks, two or three per shift.

We were only supposed to put coal in, but sometimes we'd throw in bits of rock, bits of bolt and whatever was left. Bits of wire – we put it all in.

It was dangerous work, as Les Spence recorded in his diary:

January 17, 1944. I narrowly escaped death today when I was carrying a girder, struck by trucks and all came off line just in front of me. Severely shaken. I thank God for being still alive.

May 10, 1944. Terrible tragedy this evening. Rabinovitch fell down shaft, instantly killed. Very popular fellow. Cast gloom over camp.

The POWs' state of mind was important, as Hugh Edwards remembered:

One of the things that one has to realise with prisoners of war is that we had no communication from the outside world: no post, no mail, no radio, no nothing. So how do you make up for that? Well, there would be rumours and false rumours, of course. But chaps had to somehow get around life in their own particular way. Not easy. And this is one of the things that I have never been able to convey about prisoner of war life. I don't go into the misery of it all, but the mental attitude – how did we keep going? Well, there was always tomorrow. It's very difficult to try to describe it, but each one would make up his day as he could best see. And you had no time for making other people unhappy. They were already unhappy, so why make it worse?

The very same month that the 77th boarded the hell ship – September 1943 – Ron Jones was among 280 British POWs transferred to a camp next to the huge Auschwitz concentration camp complex. An engineering worker before the war, he was going to be made to work in a camp belonging to I G Farben, the largest corporation in Europe at the start of the war.

They put us on cattle trucks and said we were going to work in a dye factory. Anyway, we got out and we were marching down the road and we saw all this barbed wire fencing and pillars, and men in pyjamas. So somebody said to one of the guards, "Who the heck are they?" And he said, "*Juden.*" "Pardon?" "Jews," he said, just like that, as though we should have known. We didn't know they were persecuting Jews, or anything. I mean, we'd been captured for over 12 months. We didn't know anything at all about it.

The POWs worked in factories with Jewish and non-Jewish forced labour. "We had to go to work. We worked six till six, Monday to Saturday. Didn't work on a Sunday."

They began to become aware of the killing centre at Auschwitz II-Birkenau, which Ron reckoned was about two kilometres away.

> Every now and then we found this terrible queer smell. So somebody said to one of the Poles that worked in the works, "What on earth is this smell?" He said, "Oh, that's the crematorium." "What do you mean, crematorium?" "Where they burn them." And eventually, of course, we realised… It must have taken me all of about three or four weeks before I really accepted that they gassed and burned the Jews.
>
> We [the POWs] used to get Red Cross parcels in – occasionally, not regular. The Germans used to pinch half of them. But if we got a parcel in, we wouldn't eat the rubbish the Germans gave us. So I had a piece of sausage one morning and I took it down the works and I gave it to one of the Jews – his name was Josef. A couple days after, he gave me a ring. He said he made it out of a steel pipe or something. A couple of weeks after, he didn't come in one morning, so I said to one of his mates, "Where's Josef this morning?" And this is exactly what he said: "Gas chamber. *Kaput.*"

Ron witnessed terrible cruelty to Jewish workers. He also saw a German soldier execute an Allied prisoner: a friend of Ron's who refused to obey the guard's order to climb an icy ladder in the factory where they were forced to work.

> In the end, [the guard] just shot him, and then he turned the gun on me and he said, "You're next." And you should see the

139

way I went up that ladder. I went up there like a blooming monkey, a bit quick. Ice or no ice. Frightened to death I was.

We used to get terrible nightmares. Thinking that one of these days, if the guards got pushed, they would put us in a chamber. We really thought this might happen.

Again, sport helped keep the POWs sane.

One Sunday afternoon, someone gave the guards a couple of cigarettes and they let us out in the field between us and the Jews' camp. So we've a regular thing now, football on a Sunday. It was only a rag ball. But very important to keep our spirits up.

Having been shot down at the end of January 1944 and had his wounds tended to by a sympathetic Luftwaffe searchlight battery, RAF wireless operator John Martin found himself at the Dulag Luft interrogation centre near Frankfurt am Main.

Straight away we were confronted by a bit of psychology. The Germans had smashed one of the windows in the front door somewhere at the front of the building and stuffed the gap with 'Window', which were strips of aluminium foil which we had dropped from our planes to foil their radar. Nobody said anything. The Germans didn't draw our attention to this or anything, but it was there. It was a psychological dig, a way of telling us that they knew all about this stuff. It was as if they were saying, "And you thought it was a well-guarded secret, didn't you? But we know everything!"

So from there we were taken off individually to be thoroughly searched by a very uncouth group of Luftwaffe airmen. I had to strip down naked, everything off. No attention being paid to any of the injuries I was suffering from. I was quite on my own. They made sure I knew that they knew a lot about us. They grabbed my battledress blouse and knew exactly where to look for the compass hidden within one of the buttons, maps and things to help us escape if we got the chance. They let me see that they knew all about them. They didn't ask me a lot of questions and were not very polite. Not at all. They were more brutal than polite!

Between long days in solitary confinement, John was brought before various officers for interrogation.

I was in the presence of this German intelligence officer who said absolutely nothing to me for several minutes. He was looking at some papers and didn't give me any attention at all. Then suddenly he turned round, and I was accused of not being a British aircrew member but in fact of being an agent who had been flying in the Lancaster to be dropped for espionage purposes.

The reason for this being that I wasn't wearing my identity discs, which I'd forgotten just before briefing for the bombing mission. I had left them hanging up in the wash place and it wasn't until we were taking off from the airfield that I remembered them. Wartime airfields were dispersed over several miles and the washing facilities were generally very primitive. But at our own station in Kirmington, I knew there was a much better ablution to be had on the main site so that's where I went. I had a good wash, taking my identity discs off, but unfortunately had left them hanging there.

At take-off it was too late to do anything about it and now this intelligence officer had picked up that my discs were missing and was making the most of it. He said that if I was a British airman, I would be wearing my identity discs. So he used it as a threat all the time and was trying to get me to prove to him that I was a British airman.

It had been drummed into us to say nothing except our name, rank and number. The German interrogator kept probing for more, then secretly summoned the guards – he must have had a bell push under his desk – and sent me back to my cell. They slammed the door shut. I was absolutely bewildered, and I wondered without these discs how was I going to prove that I was a British airman without giving something away. I know now how much psychology was put into these interrogations, which I wasn't aware of at the time.

I was back in the cell for two days before I was called in front of this same guy again. He said, "Well, if you're a British airman, then tell me where you were stationed? Where did you do your training?"

I knew I mustn't tell him anything like that as it had been drilled into us so much by our own intelligence officers – not to get into any sort of conversation at all, because they're so clever and can switch questions when you're least expecting them to do so. So once again, he dismissed me: "As far as I'm concerned, you're a spy."

John was left in his cell for a couple of days – all the while fearing he would be shot as a spy.

The next time I was called for interrogation, I didn't realise at first that I was being taken to a different place until they actually opened the door. I was met by a different intelligence officer, who had a totally different attitude. To me, he was quite friendly and he said, "We are both wireless people, technicians, so we understand each other, don't we?"

He then suddenly asked, "Were you carrying 'Fishpond'?"

This was a new visual radar display set in a grey box with a circular screen, which we were carrying to detect enemy fighters coming up from behind. We already had what we called the 'Monica' radar, but this was more advanced. Fishpond gave a blip, blip, blip, blip, blip noise and we could actually see the aircraft that it had picked up, so we were then able to give this direction to our gunners as to where the aircraft was coming from, and whether it was up or down. It was quite a good innovation but was supposed to be absolutely dead top secret. In fact, on the station, we had been told in the demonstration of Fishpond given by the RAF, "You mustn't breathe a word of this outside."

So here was this German intelligence officer now confronting me with it all. And then he suddenly says, "Oh you're not giving away any secrets. Come with me!"

And he took me into another room. And there was the Fishpond set, up and working. They then gave me a demonstration of its qualities. So that was psychology being piled on to me, I'm sure.

Anyway, he asked me another couple of things, but all the time he kept a quite friendly attitude, at least compared with the first interrogator. I was sent back to my cell from there, which was followed by another two or three sessions with the first interrogator, and he said once again, "Well, if you are RAF as you claim to be, then tell me where you were stationed and where you were trained."

Well, again, I couldn't tell him that. Then suddenly he produced this great book and flung it across the table at me.

"You're not giving away any secrets – look in there."

And I started to look at it and I realised that in this book were the names of all the RAF stations in Great Britain and what units or squadrons were stationed there. My heart sank, but just then his telephone rang. He had to take his eyes off me while he answered that. So I took this opportunity to flip through the book to see if there were these two new airfields that I knew about, which had not been in commission for very long. I saw that they weren't in the book and that gave me a bit of confidence. I thought, 'Well, he doesn't know everything, then!' But anyway, this telephone call must have been more important than him grilling me, for the next thing, the guards opened the door and took me back to my cell.

More interrogations followed, then after nine more days…

...the [cell] door was flung open and guards told me to pick up my belongings. I thought, 'This is it. I'm off to be shot.'

The Dulag Luft was a maze of corridors, and I went along several of these corridors and didn't have the slightest idea where I was. And I thought, 'Shortly, I'm going to be in front of the Gestapo.' Then suddenly we came to a big door, which looked like an exit door to the outside.

'Good Lord, they're going to shoot me here. They're going to shoot me in a yard outside this door,' I thought to myself.

But when the doors opened fully, it wasn't a yard at all, but was quite a large room which was full of Allied airmen, joking, smoking cigarettes. I was mightily relieved and immediately reassured that my interrogation was now over. I was in the clear now and would be on my way soon to a prison camp.

After successfully taking their D-Day objective of Douvres, Idwal Symonds' unit – 46 Commando – moved south. But on 11 June, the luck that had seen Idwal through D-Day ran out.

We were advancing through a cornfield with two Canadian tanks supporting us. Then, all of a sudden, the Canadians disappeared, and we realised German tanks were following the same tracks as the Canadians, because they knew they would be mine-free. They were supported by infantry of the 12th SS Division. And I was taken prisoner.

Idwal and about 20 comrades were captured in the cornfield. They faced an uncertain future: in 1942, Hitler had ordered that any Commandos who were captured should be shot.

On more or less the day I was taken prisoner, a very pompous SS officer came up and said, "On the instruction of my Führer, Adolf Hitler, I have to tell you that you are to be shot because you are Commando."

I was under sentence of death for, I think, 18 days. They didn't give me much food, so I was more hungry than worried about being shot – and I'm not exaggerating when I say that. The objective was to weaken you, I presume. We were less trouble if we were very hungry, and we were very, very hungry. And then we were suddenly forced to march south into German territory.

Idwal and the other prisoners eventually reached Chartres.

And there an SS officer came and said, "On the orders of the Führer, you're not to be shot because you were fighting as infantry." Very decent of him! And this is all for a little boy from Caernarfon!

The Commandos were then loaded onto a bus and driven through the centre of Paris, "for the Parisians to see us, in effect". They then travelled by train and lorry to Trier in the Moselle Valley, then eventually to Bremen. There, Idwal was to be a prisoner of the German Navy at the Marlag und Milag Nord prison camp complex. The guards there were not physically cruel, but food was short and the prisoners grew weak throughout the autumn and winter of 1944.

We had a circular stove standing in the middle of the room. But the stove could only be used to boil the kettle and once you'd boiled the kettle and had some tea or coffee or soup – whatever you could get your hands on – the heat was turned off. We spent a lot of time lying down. You might call it rest; I call it weakness.

John Martin remembered leaving Dulag Luft for a prison camp:

That afternoon, we were taken off to a railway siding where this long freight train was waiting. One of the trucks on the train had been fitted out specially to take us. It was very well fortified with barbed wire, and partitioned, so we were shut into the end section of this truck. The guards occupied the space by the only exit doors, so there was no chance of escaping.

The next day, because the doors were slid open a little bit, there were enough clues to indicate that we were headed northwards and most likely to northern Germany. The journey took a long time because quite frequently we were stopped and put into a siding whilst the more important trains, carrying things like field guns, bustled past us, because they had top priority.

So, having cheated almost certain death, then survived a potential attack by German civilians who had only been held back by his protective guards, intense interrogation and the very real fear of being shot as a spy, John Martin was transported to a POW camp in East Prussia.

Eventually we arrived at Stalag Luft VI, which was in Heydekrug. We were marched about a mile from the railway station to the prison camp. And that was the first idea of what we were going into. It was a very heavily guarded, barbed wire place. Absolutely impregnable either for getting in or getting out of it. The compound, which was the part of the camp that we were put in, was full mostly of American aircrew and there were only a few British airmen in there.

In those days, we had never previously met real Americans in the flesh – at least I hadn't. We expected them to be quite different to us because all we knew about them was what we saw on the American films, and that they were rich, and all got big cars, with very good-looking girlfriends. In fact, they were no different to us. When you were talking to them, you realised they only did ordinary jobs like us: clerks, plumbers and fitters, and that sort of thing.

We learnt to play their ball games, such as hardball and softball. But they were a bit different from us in that respect, as they tried to apply psychology, like shouting all sorts of insults at the man holding the bat, hoping that he would miss the ball being thrown, which was something we would never do in cricket. Oh no, we're British!

We got used to the little food because at that time, in the spring of 1944, the British Red Cross parcels were still quite evident, and we regularly had one parcel a week. Whilst the parcels didn't stop us from being hungry, they did stop us from starving and so we were most grateful for these parcels. The parcels contained things like a quarter-pound packet of tea, tin of sausages, perhaps a tin of meat, tin of salmon. They varied a bit, which was a good thing.

But as the war went on, the Red Cross parcels became more and more scarce, and after they stopped, we were having to rely on only the very meagre German rations. We wouldn't have lived much longer had we not been liberated, I don't think.

The prisoners were able to receive some news from home.

There was a [hidden] radio set in the camp, but we had more sense than to ask where it was, and the less known about its location, the better. The listener would write down the BBC news on a piece of paper and then it would be taken around and read out in each of the barracks.

The guy who came around the barracks to read the BBC news was very well spoken, with the quality of a BBC announcer. As a precaution, he had another sheet containing the German news with him, so if the Germans came into the barracks, he would quickly slide the BBC paper underneath the German news, so it was hidden and it would appear that he was reading out the German news, which of course was all propaganda.

After several months, and with the Allies making strong headway across northern Europe, John and his friend David Alletson were shipped out of Stalag Luft VI, northwards to Stalag XI-B Fallingbostel in north-western Germany.

[First] we went to this huge camp in Poland which was one side of a river, and we were very glad of having much more room to walk around in. The weather was warmer, but the food got scarcer and scarcer. We had not been there that long before we were hustled up again because we could hear the Russian guns in the distance, so we knew that the Russians weren't far off from there.

We were then brought back into Germany, 30 miles north of Hanover, into a long and a very huge area where there were several camps which were not very big, scattered around this place called Fallingbostel, which was the name of the town. But things got worse and worse after we got there.

Certainly, no food parcels at all. It went from getting half a food parcel to a quarter parcel. Then they disappeared altogether. It wasn't that the Red Cross parcels weren't being shipped from Canada, America and Britain. It was because they were being blown off the railways in Germany, vehicles on the road were attacked, and the camp Commandant admitted this to us. We didn't know whether to treat this news as being a good thing or a bad thing. Of course, we had fantastic air power superiority towards the end of the war.

What would have happened without the Red Cross parcels up to then was that we would have starved, and this starvation would have led to disease which would have been rampant throughout the camp. And, you know, I think that would have been the end of us – and liberation, when it came, saved our lives.

In this camp, we lost track of what was really going on with the war. Much earlier, in September 1944, we did hear about the taking of the bridge at Arnhem and all thought that in another week we'd be free, as we would be liberated. But, of course, although they took the bridge, which was a marvellous operation, the British Army couldn't get up to relieve them and after a bitter fight, the bridge was surrendered back to the Germans. And at the time, that news was a terrible disappointment for us.

Having had his life saved by the German medic in the woods in the Netherlands, Charles Ackerman received medical treatment for the grenade wounds to his legs.

Charles was then transported by train at night, to avoid Allied bombing, to Stalag XI-B, north of Hanover – the same camp to which John Martin had been sent. The train wagon had a milk churn filled with water, but little to eat. Some German civilians handed potatoes into the train when it stopped in a siding.

It was rough. We had nothing. I know the poor buggers from the BEF [British Expeditionary Force] were POWs for four and a half, five years before I got there, but they were having a Red Cross parcel every week. But we got there and then the Arnhem boys got there, and it was one between six, one between eight, one between twelve. It wasn't worth bleeding having.

I made pals with a big Scots Guardsman. Now, I was barely 19. And he said, "We'll stick together, Taff, I'll see you through this." He was a good man to have by your side, like, you know.

A Sergeant Major brought a group of Welshmen together. Charles remembered:

He said, "Right now, I got the six of you together. They always say if you get three or four Welshmen, you've got a choir. Well, I've got six, so I'm hoping to get some good singers off you. It's the RSM [Regimental Sergeant Major]'s birthday on Christmas morning, and I've fixed it up with the German guards for you to sing.

The little choir went to the RSM's hut a minute after midnight and sang '*Ar Hyd y Nos*'. After a while it was quiet, and the door opened and we could see the RSM was crying. "Oh, good God," he said, "Thank you so much. I can't let you go without giving you a present."

So we came out with these Russian cigarettes. Well, I was smoking then, and you couldn't get them because the [Red Cross] parcels weren't big enough. Back in the barrack room, I lit one up and thought, 'I can't smoke these, they smell like horseshit – horrible.' My mate said, "What's the matter, Ack?" "Oh, I can't smoke that." My mate asked for it. "I don't care what it is, I need a smoke." I gave them all away.

Life got worse for Charles when large trucks pulled into the POW camp and he and others were loaded aboard. Their destination was a lead mine in the Harz Mountains in central Germany.

We were right up in the mountains – it was bloody cold! We were put on two shifts: 12-hour shifts, days and nights. The French would bore the holes for the Germans. Then the Germans would come along and put the padding in it, then the gunpowder, the dynamite, whatever. Then more padding. Then: '*Achtung! Achtung!*'

Now, you had your leather helmet and a lamp. One day they blasted so much that it blew our lights out! The darkness was horrible. All I could do was tap the bloody steel rods with all the electric things going through, until somebody came up to find us. Even now, I can't stand being in enclosed places.

14

The Battle of the Bulge

"All the Yanks were so trigger-happy because the
Germans had been dressing in American uniforms,
infiltrating their lines and causing havoc… and me in the
pitch dark on a motorcycle, coming up a lane all on my
own, with a helmet very similar to a German front view."

GORDON PRIME

IN DECEMBER 1944, Nick Archdale and the 7th (Light
Infantry) Parachute Battalion were in England, preparing for
the season of peace and goodwill.

We were on a night exercise and came back at about two
o'clock in the morning to find frantic goings on: we'd been
ordered to move the following morning – Christmas Eve, I
think it was – for Belgium, to help the Americans stop the
breakthrough in the Ardennes.

And so we abandoned Christmas dinner and packed up
in lorries and set off across the Channel by ferry. We arrived
at Dieppe and did a long journey into the Ardennes – the
town of Namur. And from there, we were on foot. We were
dropped off in the snow and told, "Last man, last round, and
here you stay."

It was bitterly cold. We learnt very quickly that you
could keep warm by digging a hole in the snow and putting
something over the top. And I always remember my boys

breaking the ice with a pick to get water to shave in the
following morning. Of course, everybody shaved always
in those days – there was no two-day stubble or anything
like that! Nobody ever gave way to not keeping either your
weapon or yourself clean.

We were right in the hills and it was beautiful. Lovely
nights of bright moonlight and deep snow, crisp on top. On
patrol, we dressed up in sheets we'd got out of Belgian houses
– we sewed them over our uniforms so we couldn't be seen in
the snow. And patrolling on the snow was really rather fun in
the pine woods.

But the Germans did not attack.

By that stage, they had run out of petrol completely. And
I remember very well looking down in a little valley and
there was a line of German tanks, stationary, because they'd
absolutely run out. They literally came to a standstill because
their petrol supply had not caught up with them.

Despatch rider Gordon Prime stated:

I call it the Ardennes Battle, when von Rundstedt broke
through the Ardennes Forest and, of course, the Americans
were very thinly placed there... young rookies who hadn't got
a clue, and they just decimated them, and we sent some of
our boys up there.

This particular night, I'd got to go up there and take a
message. I eventually got there – terrible snow and horrible
night, pitch black – and prior to that, all the Yanks were
so trigger-happy because the Germans had been dressing
in American uniforms, infiltrating their lines and causing
havoc. And of course, they were all trigger-happy as hell and
me in the pitch dark on a motorcycle, coming up a lane all on
my own, with a helmet very similar to a German front view.

And these [American troops] were jumping out: "Halt, who goes there?" I had to explain who I was. In the end I thought, 'Blow this,' and I found a big log on the side of the road and I lay on it and went to sleep, with my crash helmet as a pillow.

I woke up and it was just getting light. And I remember, a V1 went over... woke me up, I think. Anyway, I was alright then, and I got back. I said, "I was more frightened of the Yanks, that night, than the Germans!" They were all so trigger-happy, you know.

Early in 1945, Royal Engineer Vernon Parry, of Prestatyn, was based outside of Brussels but was given a special treat: two days' leave in Paris.

[We had] two days on the Champs-Élysées and in the George V [hotel] and it was nearly all free. The Glenn Miller Orchestra was there, although of course Glenn Miller was missing by then.

I do remember the first meal and it was unbelievable: a tablecloth, beautiful chairs and everything. You had to take what they gave you, no choice. And the girl brought us a salad and I remember this lad saying to me, "Have you ever had a salad like this, with sultanas on the carrots? Grated carrots! I'm going to tell my mum when I get home," he said.

The next day they took us to see the Eiffel Tower. We were not allowed up the tower, but we all went and touched the base of it.

And then on the day we were leaving to go back, they gave us a carrier bag with sandwiches, an apple, an orange and, I think, a bottle of lemonade. We all got on the lorry to go back and after an hour we all wanted the toilet, so we stopped somewhere in France and we all went to the nearest hedge.

I am standing there and an American soldier put his arms up on the other side of the hedge, "I give up, I give up," he said.

153

We started talking, then the lorry driver said, "For God's sake, don't hang about with a deserter because there are American patrols and this is the big highway."

We had a Sergeant with us. "What's the matter? Where do you want to go, son?" "Home." "Where's home?" "Alabama." "Oh, well, we can't take you to Alabama," he said, "but we'll get you from here. Come on, lads, get him up!"

We gave him some food, cigarettes and money, but what were we going to do with him? We couldn't take him back to the camp – we'd get into trouble. So the lorry driver decided, "I'll make a detour. We'll drop him on the outskirts of a village and hope that he can get help." That's what we did. We were worried if the Americans did catch him, he would be court martialled, maybe executed. Afterwards we often wondered what happened to him.

Gordon Prime remembered:

We went back to a place called Breda in Holland. We were there for some time. 1 January 1945, remember it well. We'd spent Christmas there. New Year's Day, just after breakfast, we heard all this noise and banging going on and all these German aircraft overhead. 1,000 feet, 500 feet high: bombers, fighters, all heading to Belgium, towards Brussels. It appears they were bombing Brussels Airport [known then as Melsbroek] or something, and they'd got to come back so we were waiting for them.

Next field to us was the Royal Air Force Regiment and they'd got anti-tank Bofors guns. They were waiting for these and we saw this Focke-Wulf 190 – the only one I saw, believe it or not – heading towards us, and they started bashing away with this gun. Must have been 500 feet and I thought, 'Good God, they've shot his tail off!' Something flew off the back and I looked again and the thing went on smoking and flaming, and I looked again and this thing, it had come off, it started to white stream behind it. And the pilot had actually jumped out at that height, and must have pulled his chute, but he hit the ground and it killed him stone dead. And the old Focke-Wulf 190 hit the ground, and the engine flew out like a comet and caught fire. Anyway, we went over and poor devil, we wrapped him with his parachute, But as I say, he jumped out at that height – why? No ejector seat in those days. But he thought he had a chance, you know?

The Rhine Crossing and the War in the Pacific

Syd Daw's Catholic faith remained important to him during his war service.

> I went to mass, in fact, the day we crossed the Rhine – 24 March 1945. This priest came along, and we had a little table in the middle of a field, a little altar. There were seven of us, I think; seven or eight. And I was given a little picture and a note saying that I attended mass that day with the British Army of the Rhine – or the BLA, as I think it was then: the British Liberation Army. Yes, that was a nice little memory.

Did Syd find any moral issue with his role of sniper?

> In the war, you just get on with things. If you think that somebody is going to kill you, you're going to do something about it, aren't you? People have said to me, "What's it like to shoot somebody?" I said, "You're not taught to shoot somebody, you're taught to defend yourself." That's my way of looking at it. You're taught to defend yourself, that's the best way to think of it, isn't it?

As the Allies prepared to cross the Rhine, Iori Lewis, the gun commander, had received extra training… in mine clearance.

They sent me up with 12 men to clear the mines. Luckily, they were large mines – teller mines, like a big plate.

And what was it like to clear a minefield?

Ah, dodgy! The trouble with the mines is often they'd booby-trap them to another small mine, an anti-personnel. Luckily we had none of that, but I was trained to do it anyway. I could dismantle a booby trap.

We cleared a site to put the guns in there on the second day, and there were bullets flying about from a little wooded area. So we did an encircling movement – two men that side, two men the other – and we got behind this wood and there were kids there, about 12 years old, firing these rifles. Every time they fired, they staggered back about 12 yards, I think. Just four young kids, 12 years old. We just took the guns off them, gave them a slap and told them to go home.

Iori now watched as the Allies laid down smokescreens along the Rhine for days to disguise their build-up to an assault across the river. When the time came for the assault, Iori spent two days providing a barrage on the German troops to the east of the river.

The 7th (Light Infantry) Parachute Battalion had been retrained and reinforced in time for the crossing of the Rhine. As on D-Day, they would be dropping behind enemy lines. Nick Archdale flew with an American pilot in a Dakota.

He was a marvellous pilot. He showed me a photograph before we took off and asked me where I wanted to land. I put my finger on a little hedge crossing, and he dropped us, and I landed within yards of that!

But, poor chap, I don't know whether he survived or not because I was standing in the doorway of our Dakota and the left port engine was on fire – it had been hit by anti-aircraft fire. And he didn't deviate at all, he kept on an absolutely steady course until he dropped us out. And I don't know what happened after that. Brave man. And I landed, as I say, within yards of where I'd said I wanted to land.

We landed on the east of the Rhine, a few miles inland, and we didn't have a bad time of it – a lot of anti-aircraft fire and so on, but the glider boys who came in later had a dreadful time because the information was very bad and there were far more German anti-aircraft guns than we expected. And a lot of the gliders were shot down in the air, with no defence at all, and they really had an awful time.

Nick and his battalion quickly found themselves in a headlong rush across Germany. They were accompanied by two American airborne divisions, led by General Matt Ridgway.

He was determined that we were going to lead the advance across Germany, which we did really, and we set off at breakneck speed. We'd grab anything we could get hold of – bicycles, old cars, anything – to keep going.
As we approached the River Elbe, General Ridgway called together all the officers in a big gymnasium. He said, "My orders are: bum on to the Elbe." He pronounced it 'LB' – 'Bum on to the LB.' And so we just bummed on to the LB!

It was very exciting. We just went non-stop, with occasional small battles, not real stiff resistance. And we then made it directly up to the Baltic, where we met a German cavalry regiment, still with horses, who were all surrendering. I got a jolly good little horse off the commanding officer.

Despatch rider Gordon Prime remembered:

We'd got to go up to the Reichswald Forest... through the Siegfried Line into Germany, alongside the First Canadian Army, 51st Highland Division and the Royal Welch Fusiliers.

157

7 February was my birthday: I was 21. And I think it was the 6th, the day before, which was the day that the battle started, and it was still frost and snow.

We advanced up into the forest and within a couple of days, everything's thawed out – mud, and horrible. I tried to ride a motorcycle through all that mud and filth and that. Hell of a battle it was – they wouldn't give in. We eventually got up as far as Kleve. The next place was called Goch and that had been bombed with these damn earthquake bombs or whatever, because the roads were just impassable. It was like going round the wall of death on the motorbike. We carried on again to a place called Kevelaer, and we stopped there. By this time, they'd discovered Belsen. I'll always remember a report in the newspapers... Belsen, Dachau and all.

We were in this farmhouse we took over – chucked the Germans out – and this particular night, Bert and I were on duty and our headquarters were back at Goch about 20 miles back, and the telephone lines went down. Shelled, or a tank ran over them, and we lost communication. One of the DRs [despatch riders] would have to go back to headquarters to communicate [with them]. So we tossed a coin. I lost, so I had to go back.

But I went back the next morning and they said, "Your mate copped it last night." It would have been me. Poor old Bert. Got blown up.

Fred Seal's operational service covered the final months of the air war. He was a bomb-aimer on a Liberator bomber from 70 Squadron.

Our first raids were on Austria and then Yugoslavia. We bombed marshalling yards or any troop concentrations, railway junctions – anything to do with transport.

And the last mission the group did was when we bombed Hitler's Berchtesgaden.

I wasn't really scared. Because once I got in the bomb bay, I'm looking out and haven't got time to be frightened; I'm just hoping that nobody is going to come up and have a pop at us. All I knew was, it was a job I was doing. If I come back, I come back. If I didn't come back, I got killed. And that was the attitude a lot of airmen had to take, yes.

In the Far East, the war against Japan was hotting up considerably, the Japanese seeking increasingly desperately to halt a tidal wave of aerial attacks from the British and American Fleets in the Pacific. At the forefront of the British Pacific Fleet on HMS *Formidable* was 848 NAS Air Mechanic Ernest Gane, who hailed from Pontllanfraith, near Blackwood. The squadron was equipped with 18 American-built Grumman Avengers, and Ernest worked on the Avengers' engines.

On 4 May the deck park of 11 of 848 NAS's Avengers were moved forward to allow the Corsairs returning from sortie to land on the deck. At 11.31, without warning, a Japanese Mitsubishi A6M Zero fighter attacked. The Zero strafed the flight deck before any of *Formidable*'s guns could open fire, then turned sharply to drop its bomb, and dived into the forward flight deck. The ship had already turned hard to starboard, but it all happened far too quickly to avoid the violent attack. Just before hitting the base of the ship's Island (the command centre for the flight-deck), the Zero had blown up, having been caught in the blast of its own bomb.

The explosions created a large hole in the flight deck of 24 feet x 20 feet, x 2 feet deep. Two officers and six ratings were killed, with 55 other crewmen injured, many of whom were caught by shrapnel, which had peppered the ship's Island. One Avenger was blown clean over the side, and another was on fire. Seven Avengers and a Corsair which were damaged beyond repair were dumped over the side. The fires raged on the deck for a further 25 minutes before being extinguished. Ernest Gane was lucky, and survived uninjured.

15

Belsen and Liberation

"And I looked down the road a little bit further,
at the far end again, and there was a big pile, and
I thought it had been like a theatre – you know,
dummies, discarded dummies. But it wasn't that.
There was a heap of bodies."

GLYN JAMES

IN APRIL 1945, Glyn James of the RASC [Royal Army Service
Corps] was in northern Germany.

Everything was in a rush. We were trying to get as far
forward as we possibly could. My driver and I had a little
Austin 8 staff car, and I was trying to get into HQ as quickly
as possible.

But, anyway, our car broke down. And as much as my
driver tried to mend it, he couldn't do it. The next thing that
came past was a tank, and I said, "Can you take us forward,
until we meet someone we can get in with?"

So we jumped on the top. And they had this camouflage
netting on the tank but they'd put it too near the exhaust. And
the thing went on fire. And, of course, there were German
people each side of the road there, and we were saying,
"*Schnell, schnell, Wasser, Wasser!*" Which they did: they
brought out a lot of water and they chucked this water over
the burning camouflage nets and put it out.

One of them was a very elderly man, and he could speak a little bit of English, and he said, "Are you going down to the camp?" And I said, "Well, what camp is this?" "Bergen-Belsen," he said. I said, "I don't know anything about Bergen-Belsen."

The following day, Glyn requisitioned a 15-cwt lorry and, together with six or seven others, headed off in the direction the elderly man had pointed.

We made our way, as he told us, down this nice, wooded valley, roads only wide enough really for, say, two lines of traffic. When we got there, there were some big gates, open gates, and on the left-hand side was a building which looked exactly like an office block. I didn't know what was there. I didn't know what to expect. So I took my Sten gun, ran up the steps, smashed open the door and there was a bloke there in a civilian suit and he put his hands up. I said, "Who are you? What are you?" He couldn't answer – he was speaking in German.

I ran down the far end and there was one set of stairs going that way, another set of stairs going that way. So I took the right-hand ones. I ran up these steps and there was about five or six offices on the right-hand side.

I went to the first one and I think I must have only just missed this bloke by not very long because the photographs of his family were on his desk and it was Kramer, who was the boss of Belsen camp. He'd left everything on his desk.

Glyn turned and went back outside.

We couldn't afford to have a good look round or anything like that because we had to go forward all the time, so I raced downstairs and I thought, 'Well, I can go down the end there, there's some cages down there,' which I could see.

I was running down; there were these cages on the right-hand side there. When I got there, there were people inside them – in singles. But they couldn't understand me and I couldn't understand them. And they were putting their hands in between the holes of the netting and just looking at me, you see.

And I looked down the road a little bit further, at the far end again, and there was a big pile, and I thought it had been like a theatre – you know, dummies, discarded dummies. But it wasn't that. There was a heap of bodies. And what was most startling again, of course, was that I could see some children, playing about, belonging either to the people that worked in the camp, or not... Well, of course, that was enough for me. I couldn't do anything else. I thought, well, the best thing to do was to go back and report exactly what I've seen.

So I made my way back, of course, and reported it in order for someone else with more time to look at it. Our job was to keep moving on.

But, well, I'd never seen or heard of anything like it... There was some mention about camps, but I certainly didn't expect anything like I saw, because I didn't think, to be honest, that someone could be so cruel to someone else. You know, what was the idea? What had they done? You know, because they were human beings... They didn't deserve that.

Charles Ackerman's POW camp in the Harz Mountains was cleared for what became known as the 'Long March', as the Germans sought to move west with their prisoners. They joined a column of prisoners and their guards who had started their journey from near the Polish border.

The guards all wanted to get out of the way, because if the Russians found our camp and found the way the Germans treated the Russian POWs... Well, they were treated worse than dogs. They had nothing. You'd hardly believe human beings would do things like that to other human beings.

We were marching about three days, four nights. Sleeping in barns, whatever, eating raw swedes.

By the time they got to Magdeburg, they could hear the battles in the west.

Next day, all of the guards had gone. So we heard some rumbling, and it was the Americans, with their jeeps. Scouts. "All right, guys," he said. "The Americans are here. The war is over for you guys."

And he had these K-rations, boxes of K-rations, enough to feed four men. So we were scoffing it down, all this tinned ham and all. And our stomach was so small, we couldn't take it. We were vomiting. He was chucking out these cigarettes. "We gotta move on, guys," he said. "We're just scouting up ahead, but don't worry, the big stuff is coming behind."

Charles and his Scottish friend found a house and got some sleep. The next morning, the full force of the American Army swept through.

At Stalag XI-B at Fallingbostel, the British Army arrived to liberate the camp. John Martin remembered:

When eventually liberation did come [on 16 April 1945], it was quite different to what we thought it was going to be. It was so well organised. Nobody was marching or walking. They all had transport of some sort, either in a small little vehicle or in a larger lorry. The Army had really got the thing under control and although the progress wasn't fast, it was steady and sure.

But because we weren't physically well, having lost a lot of weight due to the lack of food over a sustained period, we were strongly advised to stop within the prison camp, where they could look after us. We were told not to try to go out because of the situation outside of the camp area, where there were still pockets of German resistance who wouldn't surrender. They were fanatics. We had a couple of nasty experiences, partly because some POWs didn't do what they were told to and stop in the camp, and even after that we came across a couple of difficult situations.

Then after we had been liberated for a few days, things seemed to have quietened down. Around six of us decided, "Let's go and see if we can get some eggs." So we went out of the camp and found a farm, threatened the farmer and got about half a dozen eggs. On the way back there was a copse, a plantation of young trees, and suddenly coming out of the copse were these armed German soldiers. We of course didn't have any arms, so we got as low to the ground as we could possibly get.

But we didn't need to worry, because following these young Germans were the British, armed with their Tommy guns. But then again, we had to be very careful, as how would the British soldiers know who we were? We slowly got up, shouting out who we were. Once they realised that we were British POWs, they gave us bars of chocolate.

I was talking to their Corporal about what things were like in the prison camp. Suddenly he took off his machine gun and handed it to me and said, "Here, bump this lot off." I couldn't do that. "Go on," he insisted. "Nobody knows we've got them." He wanted me to mow this lot down in cold blood. I didn't, though.

16

War's End

"They said the war had finished, and I do remember
we had a lovely breakfast that day – tinned American
bacon, dried egg, beans – and the Corporal cook said,
'Now, lads, there's a treat for you today: I've warmed
your milk for your shredded wheat.'"

VERNON PARRY

The end of the war in Europe: 8 May 1945

Syd Daw from Cardiff was in Germany with the 52nd (Lowland)
Infantry Division when the end of the war was announced.

When the war ended, I was in Bremen and they were still
firing bullets and God knows what, shells and all sorts of
things. And we captured some young lads, some Hitler
Youth who still wanted to go on killing people. None of them
would say anything. And there was one tall lad who had a
Hitler Youth knife with a swastika on it and *Blut und Ehre*:
'blood and honour'. He was a big lad and the Sergeant Major
gave him a little smack – only a little slap across the face,
you know – and had him crying. So the others opened their
mouths then; they were ready to talk then, when they saw
this big lad wasn't as clever as he thought he was. Sad.

Royal Engineer Vernon Parry from Prestatyn, who had come
ashore at Normandy a few weeks after D-Day and served

in Caen, Brussels and Eindhoven, found himself in a small German town.

> They said the war had finished, and I do remember we had a lovely breakfast that day – tinned American bacon, dried egg, beans – and the Corporal cook said, "Now, lads, there's a treat for you today: I've warmed your milk for your shredded wheat."
>
> So we thought, 'Now we'll have a fairly easy time,' but the old Major said, "Now, boys. You've been on the go for 11 months and you're a bit ragged. I think you'll have to teach these Germans how smart the British Army is. Smarten yourselves up. And I think we should do some drill!"
>
> And we did drill in this road for about an hour. A beautiful road with green trees on one side and an 88-millimetre gun on the other end of it. Afterwards he said we could have the afternoon off, and said, "Now, then: you must not fraternise, you must not speak to any Germans, you must not accept any hospitality; but you can give the children chocolate. You must go out in a minimum of four because we don't know what their reaction is going to be."

Vernon and three others headed out, armed with a rifle and 15 rounds of ammo. As he walked, Vernon witnessed various scenes from the defeated Germany.

> We came across a block of flats – four storeys or something like that, with a play area in the front – and you could see the young women, prams and children running about and all had something out the window: towels, bed sheets, like an act of surrender. And I remember walking over there and thinking, 'Well, Adolf, you bloody started it.'
>
> Anyway, this old lady, she grabbed me by the arm because I was the nearest one to the flats, and she said, "*Russki?*" and I said, "*Nein*, English," and she kissed me on the cheek. She

was older than my grandmother. And she had a better 'tache than my grandfather.

We crossed over then and there was a shop – I think it had furniture. But there were German prisoners with one or two Scots Guards with them. Further down we came across a barbershop with a pole. I opened the door. *"Guten tag,"* he said. There was one German in his chair, having a shave, and one waiting. So I got my fags out. *"Zigaretten?"* *"Oh, danke schön. Danke schön."*

The two Germans left and then I was the first one to risk going into the black chair, and I said, *"Kleine, bitte, mein Herr,"* and he said, *"Ja, ja, verstehen, verstehen,"* and he gave me an SBS, you know – a short back and sides. And I always remember him: he had a big pair of boots, corduroy trousers and a smock, and as he finished cutting my hair he went for his brush and his boots squeaked when he was going across the shop.

Anyway, when he finished, he had a sense of humour and he wanted to give me a shave with a cut-throat razor! I said, *"Nein, nein!"*

And then my mates, they all had a haircut with him. And he was very good – he had a damn good head of hair himself. When we were leaving, it was the usual rhetoric – *"Alles ist kaputt in Deutschland,"* and all that, you know – and then we left him.

Vernon's unit was then posted to Hamburg, where they worked on the docks. In their spare time they roamed the ruined city, including a Woolworth's store with barely anything on the shelves.

One day, on a tram, a very tall German in a long leather coat said, "Can I shake your hand?" And I said, "Yes." He said, "I want to give you a message, and one day you will tell this to your grandchildren: this war should never have been. It is Miller fighting Müller, Schmidt fighting Smith, and the Russian bear is laughing. You will never forget that," he said. *"Auf Wiedersehen."*

Kemys Morgan, who had escaped from France in the summer of 1940 and by now had two operational tours under his belt, navigated a B-25 Mitchell Mk. III of 98 Squadron into Copenhagen airfield on 7 May 1945. The 98 Squadron Operational Records Book (ORB) records:

> The squadron was given the mission of flying VIPs into Copenhagen. Four crews carried out this task. The first crew arrived in Copenhagen only six hours after the city had been liberated. The crew had a rousing reception, they being the very first Royal Air Force personnel to be seen walking the streets of Copenhagen. They naturally felt proud of the fact that they belonged to the Royal Air Force.

In 1985, in discussion with his younger brother – wartime pilot Flight Lieutenant Ted Morgan – Kemys recalled that as they landed, two German staff cars drove alongside. Then through the ear-splitting cacophony inside the cockpit caused by the deafening two Wright Cyclone radial engines, pilot Ken Jarvis brought the Mitchell to a halt. The members of the Danish legation on board, who were returning to govern their country for the first time in the five years since it had been occupied and suppressed by Nazi Germany, disembarked the Mitchell and were taken away in the back of the staff cars.

A Luftwaffe sentry was posted by the aeroplane. The British crew was momentarily unsure of what to do next, and the frustration of several years of war suddenly built up and the desire to let off steam became too great. Determined not to miss out on the celebrations, Ken Jarvis in the cockpit shouted to the Luftwaffe sentry to get a staff car to the aircraft. The guard apparently didn't understand – or maybe he was just unsure and deliberately avoided the instruction. So Ken drew out his handgun, pointed it at the sentry and ordered him to fetch a staff car with driver.

The staff car duly arrived and the five-man crew piled in, and, pistol at the ready, ordered the driver to take them to the severely bomb-damaged Tivoli Gardens, where thousands of people were milling.

In their RAF battledress, they stood out like sore thumbs, for the five were the very first RAF personnel to enter the city after so many years of occupation. Slaps on the back, kisses, congratulatory shouts and waves ensued. Enjoying the adulation, they walked past a doorway, where a hand reached out and pulled Kemys into a hallway – and the crew quickly followed.

Taken into the back of the building, they entered a spacious bar, where members of the Danish resistance immediately handed them large beers. Looking around the room, they were astonished to see uniformed German personnel drinking beers too. The Danish resistance sang the Danish national anthem (though which of their two official national anthems, it is not known), to be followed by the Germans, who stood up at their table and sang the *'Deutschlandlied'*. The room went suddenly quiet as an expectant audience waited for the by-now boozy crew of the Mitchell to sing 'God Save The King'. Unsurprisingly, Kemys had little recollection of what occurred later, other than the crew of the Mitchell returning back to base the following day.

Nick Archdale and the 7th (Light Infantry) Parachute Battalion ended the war alongside soldiers of the 'Russian Bear'.

As we got to the Baltic, the war ended. We bumped into the Russians there. I was with my boys and a Russian officer arrived, inviting us to go and drink with him, so two other officers and I went off that evening. And that was very difficult, because the Russian officers were living in grand style, while the men were just in ditches and things: you know, just the opposite of what you'd expect.

We were all given little vodka cups and somebody made a toast to something or other – in Russian mostly – and then you had to drink the whole lot in one gulp. And, of course, I remember getting completely plastered because you weren't used to this sort of thing. But they seemed to be able to drink anything.

We had two or three days with the Russians and the Americans, each contributing one platoon to a sort of parade in a big castle forecourt. I was in command of the platoon representing the British Army, really. And we had a great march round and all that sort of stuff.

The end of the war did not bring the feelings that Nick expected. He was the "only officer in the battalion who was unwounded and alive right through", but...

[VE Day] wasn't a feeling of rejoicing at all, because, funnily enough, everything we'd trained for – our lives – had been devoted to what we were doing, and suddenly it was all over. And it was a feeling of slight deflation, in a way. You know, there was no sort of whooping and bonfires and things at all.

Iori Lewis was in Kiel in northern Germany with the 7th Armoured Division early in May, and his unit had been told to carry on into Denmark.

We were packing up when they announced that the war was over. It was quite a shock to the system. Didn't expect it. I can't describe it. Flummoxed – you know, it just didn't sink in. It took days to realise that the thing was finished. You felt lost. I looked at the gun and I said, "I don't need that any more."

If only it had finished a few days before, we'd have kept a few more lives, because some people were killed in the last couple of days.

Yes, it was quite a shock to the system, really. And that's where the problem started with all of us. Things were over, and you started to get nerves – reaction, I suppose. Post-traumatic stress they call it these days, isn't it? That was a problem. But we survived.

In North Weald on VE Day, WAAF plotter Pauline Penrose remembered:

We were all confined to camp, because they were concerned that there might be a last attempt by the Luftwaffe to fly over and put all their bombs on us. The last gesture, I suppose. We were confined to camp.

Decades later, Pauline wrote a letter about this which was published in the *Radio Times*. Soon after,

A girl got in touch with me, and she was in the [small contingent of] Army at North Weald. She had read my letter and she asked them for my address so she could contact me. She sent me a letter saying, 'I remember us being confined to camp' – because a lot of people wouldn't believe it, as on VE Day everybody was out celebrating and we were confined to camp!

Back in the UK, Cardiff-born Maldwyn Mills was at the Dering Lines Camp in Brecon, training as an infantryman, which involved ten weeks of Corps training followed by five weeks' Battalion training. Whilst there, VE Day was announced.

We were woken up by the joyful setting-off of smoke bombs all over the camp. In our Nissen hut, which was close to the

parade ground, two lads had found some smoke mortars and
the whole hut was smothered in green smoke. There was a
row over the mess. A pig had 'escaped' from the orchard and
someone had covered it in painted swastikas!

The prisoners in the factories and camps next to the death
camp at Auschwitz had been forced to march west. By the time
he was liberated by American soldiers, Ron Jones weighed
just seven and a half stone. He returned home to Newport to
an emotional reunion with his wife, Gwladys.

> And of all the people that were in the house waiting for me
> – my family and Glad's family – who should come out the
> back door but Gwladys. I caught hold of her – and she was
> going to the outside toilet, but she didn't go for a couple of
> hours. I wouldn't let her. I wouldn't let go of her. I remember
> the first night: she put me in the bath and started to cry,
> because I was like a boy from Belsen, you know. I said, "Oh,
> don't cry, love." I said, "I'm here in one piece. I left men out
> there that are never going to come home." But I was in a bit
> of a shocking state. Gwladys used to say, "You're not the man
> I married," because I wasn't. I was a different man altogether.

The end of the war in Japan: 15 August 1945

Liberation for the prisoners in Japan came following the
dropping of the atomic bomb on Nagasaki, a city less than 100
miles from the camp where Hugh Edwards and Les Spence
had been working as coal miners.

'We had a rather exciting morning, going down [to the
air-raid shelter] no fewer than four times,' Spence wrote on
9 August 1945. 'We saw no planes.'

Only four planes flew on the raid that had destroyed
Nagasaki, and the camp did not understand what had
happened at first. The Japanese guards were in a state of
confusion for days.

'We hear from the guards that one bomb blew up Nagasaki,' Spence wrote. 'The huge cloud we saw must have been big oil wells catching fire. We must now take over the camp.'

Hugh Edwards stated:

I have to describe to you... the war was officially over on 14 or 15 August. We were not told – we were still working until the 29th. A fortnight after. Because we were in a little village.

Suddenly we were told, "There's no more." The guards said, "All rest. No more work." Well, this went on for two days, and then we were all lined up and the Japanese Commandant came out and he stood up on the bank there, talking and saying something... and the interpreter told us that the war was over.

How did he react?

Three and a half years. Weak. Tired. Hungry. I'm not ashamed to admit I was one of a good group who shed a few tears. But they were in gratitude.

And I can see men now, looking at each other, impossible to say a word. Can't say a word. Too full up, too choked.

That's the effect that the news of freedom had.

On 18 August 1945, Les Spence's diary marked his 1,259th day as a POW. But it was more than a month before he left Camp 8.

September 21, 1945. We left camp today... I left at 8 a.m., in charge of 215 English. The whole village turned out to see us off. I was the last man to leave the camp and the first to come in. We had an uneventful train journey to Nagasaki and then we saw the result of the atomic bomb. It was simply astounding, nothing left standing for miles, everything flat and burnt out.

Hugh Edwards reflected:

> I know [the bomb] meant devastation, I know it meant a lot
> of death. But it meant our freedom. Am I being selfish? I've
> never found any alternative. I'm sorry, but I've never found
> one. I think if it had gone on and on and on, I don't know
> what would have happened to us. I don't know what would
> have happened to the country.
>
> When we came out of Nagasaki, I was suffering. My heart
> was bad as well – but don't worry, it was only a condition of
> the time – and I think my weight was somewhere around six
> and a half stone.

The former prisoners were taken by sea to San Francisco.
They then travelled east by train and boarded the *Queen Mary*
for the UK in New York on 13 November 1945.

Royal Engineer Richard Pelzer had returned to Britain in
early 1945 and quickly found himself posted to India. He was
in the Malacca Strait on the way to Singapore, en route to
India, when a senior officer came on board.

> He said, "We are cutting steam." That meant that we were
> stopping. "Our Allied friends have released the secret weapon
> on Japan," he told us. For a while, we were still on war
> footing. We knew all about the kamikaze people, and we
> wondered, 'Will they listen to the Emperor, or defy him?'

Now ordered to stay in Singapore instead of proceeding to
India, Richard's company was given a grim duty.

> They told us, "You're not going to be idle. We've taken the
> company over. You will now be a funeral company." So many
> of the Allied prisoners who got released and didn't make it.
>
> And every [former Japanese] prisoner, even civilians, was
> buried in a coffin which was made by our company. And

everyone had a military funeral. And that's the only time, then, that I had a rifle: I was a member of the firing party.

Army of Occupation in Japan

A member of the first British advance party entering Japan weeks after the atom bombs were dropped on Hiroshima and Nagasaki, Duncan Hilling spent the next nine months there.

The Royal Welch Fusiliers, Cameron Highlanders and the Dorsets reformed as the 25th Independent Infantry Brigade, to be sent out to Japan. I was fortunate: I went out with the advance party with the vehicles, including Bren Gun Carriers shipped there on small vessels, which would have been 6–7,000 tons.

There was a terrific storm and the small ship would ride to the crest of a wave and as it dropped down, the propeller screw would be out of the water, grinding away in mid-air. The cooking facilities were brilliant as an ordinary kitchen range had been welded to the deck, with a steel frame welded around it which had canvas over the top, to protect the chefs from the sun and the rain and the wind.

I remember a boy collecting his food on the ship, which was listing to such a degree that when a wave came over the top, it washed his food away. So he went back again for second helpings and the same thing happened. He shouted, "Bugger it!" and threw his plate over the side.

In charge was a Captain from the Cameron Highlanders, and he wanted to start a dance group. He said to me, "Your name is Duncan, so you've got to have some Scottish connection." I said, "None whatsoever." "Even so," he said, "You can learn to dance." I learned how to do a sword dance and perform with these other five. I wasn't very good because I couldn't dance in any shape or form, but the Captain seemed to enjoy it and it was part of the entertainment for the troops.

Eventually Duncan arrived at a former Japanese barracks just outside Hiroshima.

> We had complete freedom, given by a marvellous Major who was in charge. He just gave us the jobs we had to do, [and then] most afternoons we could travel around the area.

How did he find the civilian population? Because, of course, Japan had only recently surrendered.

> The Japanese civilian population was so different from their troops, who would have shot and just killed anybody who was their enemy. The Japanese people themselves were so friendly and accommodating – and the amount of people in Japan who could speak English! Every schoolmaster, station master, policeman could speak English – though spoken with an American accent, of course, as their main influence was from America. But you felt a welcome, and were almost made a member of the family when you visited people in Japan at that time.
>
> In the first few days of arriving, because of the freedom we had, I drove six of us into Hiroshima to see the damage there. It's indescribable, really. We went into a hospital, where people were just lying on beds. A lot of them, their skin had peeled off their faces and arms. It was a hideous sight. Lots of them were blind: the bomb had blinded them when they heard this plane overhead and looked up, which was absolutely fatal because they saw this bomb explode in mid-air right above them.
>
> One bridge had completely melted. This was the bridge over a river [in Hiroshima]. There was no building which wasn't damaged, but some of them were absolutely and totally destroyed. It was totally indescribable what we saw there.

We were not made aware of any danger from radiation, so we picked up bits and pieces and took them back to the barracks. Most of the boys who were with me died of cancer. One young boy, Bryn Mosley from Ebbw Vale, was only 35 when he died.

Had he been affected by those scenes?

I think you are bound to be affected emotionally as there is no way of really describing the real horror of seeing those patients in hospital. It's beyond description. When I go into a hospital now and see these beds spaced out nicely – those beds were almost touching and lots of them on the floor, every spare inch in the building and around the building – which was still intact – full of patients. And they died for months and months, and years afterwards.

17

Post-War and Looking Back

"Yes, I was frightened. I cried and I prayed to God.
In some places I was very frightened –
I'm not ashamed to say so."

TED OWENS

OUR VOICES OF World War Two never saw themselves as heroes. They had lived through an extraordinary time. Done their duty. Experienced things they did not want subsequent generations to see.

Speaking 68 years on, Stewart Johnson still did not wish to speak about some of his experiences on the road from Normandy to Operation Market Garden in the Netherlands.

Obviously, I came across a great number of pretty grim
scenes that I never talk about and have no intention of doing.
I've no desire to revive memories of them.

As he spoke, young people from the street where he lived passed the house. Those young people would not be able to imagine the horrors their elderly neighbour had in his mind. Stewart said:

They wouldn't have the opportunity, and I hope to goodness
they don't have it.

After the war, Stewart received a government retraining grant and worked for many years as a solicitor.

Speaking at his home in Dinas Powys, Idwal Symonds of 46 Commando, who had taken part in D-Day, said:

> When did I feel most in danger? Well, it was all danger. Apprehension of danger. The two words are linked. Because we accepted danger. And I accepted that I would probably not survive the next few days. And I hoped that they would be gentle when they told my mother that I was dead, because I expected to be killed – as a lot of my friends were. It was a fatalism, but not a morbid fatalism. A realistic fatalism, if you like.

Syd Daw spent two years working in the British Commandant's office in Berlin before coming back to Cardiff in 1947.

> Berlin was bombed, shattered. Terrible. I felt sorry for the ordinary Germany people – the non-Nazis. I found that they were so like us. Anyway, I came home and went back to work at East Moors works and the blast furnaces. A promotion had been kept open for me and I worked my way up to blast furnace manager.

Oliver Lindsay, who had been torpedoed and sunk on an Arctic convoy when he was just a teenager, said:

> My whole philosophy – if you can talk about a boy of 17 having a philosophy, I don't know – was, 'It will happen to somebody else, but it won't happen to me.'

Bomb-aimer Fred Seal reflected:

> Put it this way: if it hadn't been for the war, I wouldn't have seen South Africa or spent as many days as I did down in the

old city of Jerusalem. I did things I had never done before, never done before. All I would have done was read about them in a book.

After the war, I was called up before the CO and I went in. "Sit down, my man." I sat down. He said, "From now on, you're a civilian." He had about four different letters from people in jobs telling them that being as I was an ex-building worker, I must come back. My CO said, "You had to knock the buggers down – now go build them back up again."

So that was the end of me. And I came home in January 1946. And that's about it.

After the war, paratroop officer Nick Archdale spent decades farming at Nannerch in Flintshire. He was one of the founders of the Welsh Halfbred Sheep Society and spent time as High Sheriff of Flintshire.

I think the war altered your life completely, in a way, because the first five years – from schoolboy to 24 – you were totally occupied in this extraordinary business of war. I'd always wanted to farm, but I hadn't got any money or anything. But I wanted to get away and I ended up here, and I've had a marvellous life ever since.

Iori Lewis became President of the Royal British Legion in Aberystwyth and raised money for several charities. He noted the effect of the war on himself and others:

I can wipe things out very easily. I've got a sense of humour, as well. People asked me, "Did you get nightmares?" No. I can talk about the past, tell you all about it, but I don't dwell there. I go forward. Burnt bridges – you don't go back over burnt bridges; they are down. You can't do a thing about it. I'm that kind of person but, unfortunately, some of my friends were not. I know two who drank themselves to death

shortly after the war. Three died who were not involved in
the fighting at all – miles behind the line. They died shortly
after the war. Because the sound of battle is worse than being
in battle itself. I was in the battle, but they were not. And they
worried about us more, and that had an effect on them... the
sound of battle. But once you were in the battle, you had a
job to do. It didn't worry you. And you did the job regardless
of what was happening – shells, bombs, strafing. It's just a
case of 'Do your job or you could let the side down.' A lot of
people depend on you.

Far East POW Les Spence went on to become Chairman of
Cardiff Rugby Club and joint Secretary of Glamorgan County
Cricket Club. In 1973, as President of the Welsh Rugby
Union, he helped take a small step to heal the wounds opened
between the UK and Japan during World War Two. He formed
a firm friendship with Shiggy Konno, manager of the visiting
Japanese rugby side, and two years later he led the Wales rugby
team on a tour of Japan. As the *South Wales Echo* reported,
Les 'learned to forgive if not forget the tragedy of war'.

His friend Hugh Edwards became Revd Hugh Edwards,
a Baptist minister, based for many years in Newport. He
explained:

> I had a faith that everything was going to be alright. There
> were times of doubt, of course, but it wouldn't last very long.
> I had a deeper faith than that. I still have.

It took a long time for Ron Jones of Newport to get over being
forced to work in the factory next to the Auschwitz death camp.
Interviewed in 2017, he was asked if he still had nightmares.

> No, not now I don't. I did to start with, though. I would get
> terrible nightmares, night after night. For instance, when
> I would work nights, if I came home, Gwladys would be in

bed. I used to walk up the stairs backwards. I wouldn't walk up front-ways. There was always that fear that someone was going to put a hand on my shoulder. I don't know why, but nerves are a shocking thing. I was in a bit of a state for all of about four or five years.

In 1946 Kemys Morgan transferred to the RAF Regiment, with which he served in Malaya. In 1953 he was awarded a second Mention-in-Despatches. and his name with this award can still be seen today on a wooden shield in the RAF Regiment Heritage Centre in Bury St Edmunds. Kemys said he regretted not having transferred to the Regiment earlier, for when he did, he took to it "like a duck to water". Kemys' nephew, Hugh Morgan, is co-author of this book.

Adelaide Jarman patiently waited for John Martin to be repatriated from Germany, where he had been a POW. On his return, they were both given leave together. Looking back fondly to her days as a flight mechanic at Little Rissington in the 1940s, Adelaide said:

The girls were highly qualified and efficient at their job, and we had such a bond of friendship that we all kept in touch for decades after the war, and we were still talking aircrew all those years later!

Gordon Prime passionately believed that there should be something in the National Memorial Arboretum in Staffordshire to honour all despatch riders. Towards the end of his life, Gordon started a campaign to draw attention to this aim and even published a small print run of his wartime story, *Bash on Regardless*, to raise awareness. There is still no despatch rider memorial anywhere in the UK.

When Duncan Hilling returned home to Saundersfoot from Malaya in 1947, he was offered resettlement training in three areas: farming, shoemaking and horticulture.

I discussed this with my girlfriend [who later became his wife]. She said, "Well, my father is a farmer and my mother complains of him coming in with cow's dung, so I don't want you farming. I can't see any future in shoemaking, so that leaves only one choice – horticulture!"

It was a wise choice, for Duncan came to enjoy a very successful career in horticulture. Today he lives in Pembrokeshire, where it all started, tending to his garden.

Eric Evans eventually returned home to his family in Llanelli after having been badly injured in a B-24 crash during the campaign in Burma. He then went to work for an uncle who ran a jeweller's shop in Swansea, where he developed an expertise in repairing watches. Eric set up his own watch-repairing business, which he continued to successfully manage for the rest of his career. Eric was very proud of his service in the RAF, but said in 2019 that he was still affected by the severe physical injuries he had received during World War Two.

Having witnessed the London Blitz at close hand before becoming a WAAF plotter at frontline fighter stations, Pauline Penrose reflected in 2021:

Looking back, though, it was such an interesting time. I'm glad I did go into the Air Force. I was very lucky. My fiancé was Signals in the Air Force. He had to learn Morse Code and listen to and take down German communications. After three and a half years he got leave and came home for a fortnight. We got married, 'special licence', and then he went back to Egypt – and he'd been all over the place: Malta, Sicily.

After post-war spells as an air traffic controller in the RAF and then in civil aviation, Trevor Jones decided to return to Wales, becoming an enthusiastic member of the Cardiff branch of the Aircrew Association. It was at one of their meetings in

Whitchurch that he was amazed and delighted to see himself featuring in the film *Night Bombers*, some 40 or so years after it had been filmed by the Station Commander at RAF Hemswell, Air Commodore H I Cozens.

This unique film is the only known colour film in existence of an RAF Bomber Command raid. It supposedly depicts a raid which took place on Berlin during the winter of 1943. In the film, having landed back at base in RAF Hemswell, Trevor can be seen in the debriefing scene – as can the rest of his crew, including pilot Squadron Leader Tommy Wright. But there is one small problem, for Trevor hadn't commenced his tour of Ops by that point. So what is the explanation for this oddity?

The film reels for Cozen's *Night Bombers* are held by the Imperial War Museum. On closer inspection, they are in fact not from a raid on Berlin in 1943, but from a bombing mission dated '23.02.1945', which was carried out on the south-western German city of Pforzheim. Reference to Trevor's logbook on this date confirms his involvement on the Pforzheim sortie and explains his appearance in *Night Bombers*. It seems therefore that wartime and post-war propaganda blurred reality – but it's still a great film!

Date	Aircraft Type & No.	Pilot	Duty	Remarks	Flying Times Day/Night
23.2.45	ME 302	S/LDR Wright	Air Gunner	OPS GERMANY PFORZHEIM MODERATE FLAK. NO CLOUD	8.20

The Women's Land Army proved to be no 'easy war' for thousands of young women, as Mary Bott remembered:

I was sent to a small farm near Penparcau, where they milked 10 cows by hand. The farmer used a pony and trap to deliver the milk. I had to get up at 5.30 a.m. and after milking, I could smell the bacon and eggs. The farmer was eating them, and I was given porridge! It was exhausting – I still today don't know how I survived! By this time the war had ended and I decided to go to college, where I trained to be a teacher.

Post-war, Mary remained in Ceredigion, becoming a primary school teacher, and was honoured with an MBE for her services to volunteering, charity work and the community.

After being repatriated from Stalag XI, John Martin returned to England and went back to work in a coachbuilding company in London. He and Adelaide married in September 1945, honeymooning in Wales. John and Adelaide retired to west Wales and in 2018 John's memoir of his wartime experiences, *A Raid Over Berlin*, was published.

Pembrokeshire's last veteran of D-Day, Tony Bird, interviewed initially in 2020, remembered:

In 2015, I was invited to apply for a French decoration, and was honoured on returning from a trip abroad to find a letter from the French Embassy in London enclosing a medal and signature '*Chevalier de la Légion d'honneur*', which was a tremendous surprise – and what a really fine gesture on the part of the French, I thought.

Tony married Florence Paul, who had been in the Wrens. They had known each other from their schooldays, as Florence's brother had been a schoolmate of Tony's. It is quite remarkable that Tony *and* Florence, both Royal Navy, contributed to the D-Day Normandy landings on 6 June 1944.

After D-Day, Florence volunteered to be in the first party of Wrens to land in Normandy, undertaking cypher duties for ship movements (including her future husband Tony's corvette, HMS *Clematis*) in and out of Mulberry B on Gold Beach from the signalling station in Arromanches. As the Allies pushed the enemy back, Florence and her fellow Wrens were moved first to Calais, then to Brussels, Minden and Hamburg, and finally Berlin in 1946. Sadly, Florence died in the early 1980s.

Mary Griffiths (née Walker), who had been a teenage firefighter in Llanelli town centre, then served for four years as a WAAF, including at RAF Hemswell (where Trevor Jones also happened to be based at the same time), before demob in September 1946. Post-war, Mary returned to Llanelli, becoming a founder member of 'Llanelly' RAF Association, and was its last Chair before it disbanded some years ago.

In 1941, Don Davies and his 8-year-old twin brother, Dennis, received a personal handwritten letter from Prime Minister Winston Churchill, which Don still occasionally looks at today. Having witnessed the Swansea Blitz, the arrival of American troops in Llandybie and visits from Italian prisoners of war to the Davies family household, Don and his brother were later conscripted for National Service in the British Army, following which, Don became a senior NCO in the Territorial Army Volunteer Reserve, with whom he served for 30 years.

Interviewed in 2021, Dame Stephanie Shirley CH's achievements – as a champion of women's voices in the workplace, as a pioneer in the emerging IT industry of the 1960s to 1980s and as a philanthropist – are all the more remarkable considering the traumatic upheaval of her childhood and escape from Nazi Germany in 1939. As with Renate Collins, who came over on a Kindertransport from Prague just a few months before Dame Stephanie, like her aged just 5, one is left wondering if these traumatic early life experiences shaped a self-reliance, inner resilience and real determination to do well, but also, importantly, to treat others kindly. Two truly remarkable people.

Renate Collins was interviewed in 2024 for Age Cymru Dyfed's West Wales Veterans Archive, her humour shining through. Looking back, "being in the Valleys, we had mountains both sides of us and Dad found out [after the war] that Hess had identified one of the mountains as a good central landing place [for the Germans]." In 2019, Renate was honoured with the British Empire Medal for services to Holocaust Education, but insists, "I always say, I don't do Education – I just give my story."

Dennis Tidswell – veteran of the Battle of Britain, a shipwreck in the Med, almost three years in Malta and severe injuries in a V1 explosion when he came back to the UK – worked in insurance throughout west Wales until retirement. From his home in Pembrokeshire, Dennis decided to speak about his war for the first time in 2020, and in 2022 featured in the ITV Wales/Age Cymru Dyfed film *Greatest Generation*, alongside Mary Bott, Syd Daw and John and Adelaide Martin. He said:

> If you were to ask me why I lasted so long, I would say:
> regular moderate exercise and then, steadfastly throughout
> your life, drinking your way through every Scottish distillery.

Speaking in July 2020, Jean McKay recalled the Anderson shelter at home during the period when, as a 17-year-old, she had personally handed reports on the night's bombing to Winston Churchill.

> Ours was within a gap between three houses. It wouldn't
> have saved you from anything – though shrapnel, I suppose,
> it might have saved you from. We all used to sleep in there
> until about October, when it started to rain and it got filled
> up with water, so we went back indoors and hid under the
> dining room table!

Post-war, Jean's husband continued a career with the Met Office and they finished up in Aberporth, where Jean lived for the rest of her life.

Shortly after demob in 1946, Archie Thomas was advised by his GP to apply for a War Pension due to the severe injury he had received as a Royal Navy Beach Commando during the Invasion of Italy in 1943. Archie wryly recalled that although he did receive it for eight weeks at the time, it was only in the 1980s that he again belatedly began to receive a small War Pension. Following his wartime service, Archie returned to his pre-service career as a painter and decorator and worked for West Glamorgan County Council, and latterly at the Abbey Works in Port Talbot.

Until shortly before his death at 102, Neville Bowen's social calendar would continue to make many half his age envious. Well-known in Ammanford, he enjoyed the company of many local veterans and was universally revered by them. Neville had returned from the war to work in the mines for nearly 20 years, and then as a driver. Following retirement, he became highly proficient at turning wood on his lathe and produced beautiful pieces including pens, bowls and mushrooms, which were sold to raise money for veteran's charities.

Born in Cardiff, Maldwyn Mills witnessed many of the early air raids on the city, especially around the City Road area. Looking back in 2019, he recalled that "for anyone who had been in a World War Two German air raid, the throbbing 'zoom, zoom' beat of the engines was unmistakable". After demob, Maldwyn resumed his university studies and moved to Aberystwyth in 1959 to pursue a distinguished academic career, lecturing in English Literature at Aberystwyth University. He became a Professor of English, specialising in Middle English Romances, and retired in 2003.

In 1942, Enid Lewis (née Lloyd) became an ATS aircraft plotter, based initially in north Wales before being stationed in Chatham, Kent. While there, she witnessed the start of D-Day and took part in the VE Day celebrations held in London. Demobbed in 1946 with the rank of Lance Corporal, Enid joined the British Control Commission in Düsseldorf,

Germany, helping in the resettlement of displaced persons. Enid's daughter Jane Lewis recalls:

> During her Army career, she had 11 proposals of marriage and nearly married a Scottish pig farmer, but decided the farming life wasn't for her and accepted my father's proposal instead. When my father retired in 1979, they moved back to Carmarthen.

Enid's wartime diaries cover the whole of the war, including such important events as the Swansea Blitz and V1 Flying Bomb attacks, and have been donated by Jane to the National Library of Wales.

Looking back at the war, Ted Owens of Pembroke Dock, who died in 2023, stated:

> Any man who wasn't frightened, there was something wrong with him. Yes, I was frightened. I cried and I prayed to God. In some places I was very frightened – I'm not ashamed to say so.
>
> I didn't talk about the war until much later. Then my war story came out.
>
> On my first trip back to Normandy, I met the Queen there and she said to me, "Did you fight in this area?" I said, "I was on Sword Beach. I was badly wounded on the beach and I got wounded twice again after that." "Oh," she said, "You went over the top once too often, didn't you?" I said, "Yes, Ma'am. I don't think they liked my face," and she busted out laughing.

Brothers and bomber pilots John and Doug Evans from Goodwick always remembered the comrades who never returned. In 2012, sitting in the living room of his home near Nottingham, beneath a painting of his Halifax aircraft, John stated:

During the war, Bomber Command lost 55,000 brave men and, whatever the rights and wrongs of the campaign, at least their heroism and self-sacrifice should be remembered and honoured.

When will the world come to its senses about the futility of war, I wonder?

After the war, Richard Pelzer – the man who secretly cleared obstacles on Gold Beach in the hours before the D-Day invasion began – continued to work in the construction industry until he broke his back in a fall. He took great pride in telling local schoolchildren about his war and in 2016 he was awarded the *Légion d'honneur* by the French government. He said:

You put [my story] in a book and some people would read it and say, "What a bloody good fiction book." But it's true and it's my story.

Index

Also from Y Lolfa:

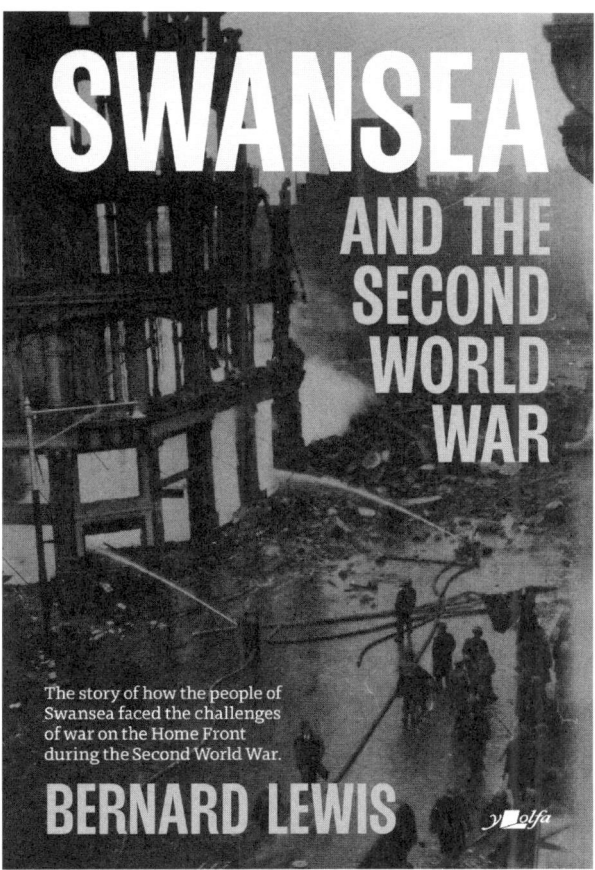

£14.99

A testament to life on the Home Front in Swansea over the course of World War Two. It focuses especially on the experiences of ordinary people in a town whose port and industries were key targets for the Nazis.

Wales' Unknown Hero:
Soldier, Spy, Monk

THE LIFE OF HENRY COOMBE-TENNANT, MC, OF NEATH

BERNARD LEWIS

£12.99

The astonishing story of Henry Coombe-Tennant of Neath.
He escaped his World War Two POW camp, joined
Special Forces and aided the French Resistance,
before working for the British Secret Service in Baghdad
and ending his days as a Benedictine monk!

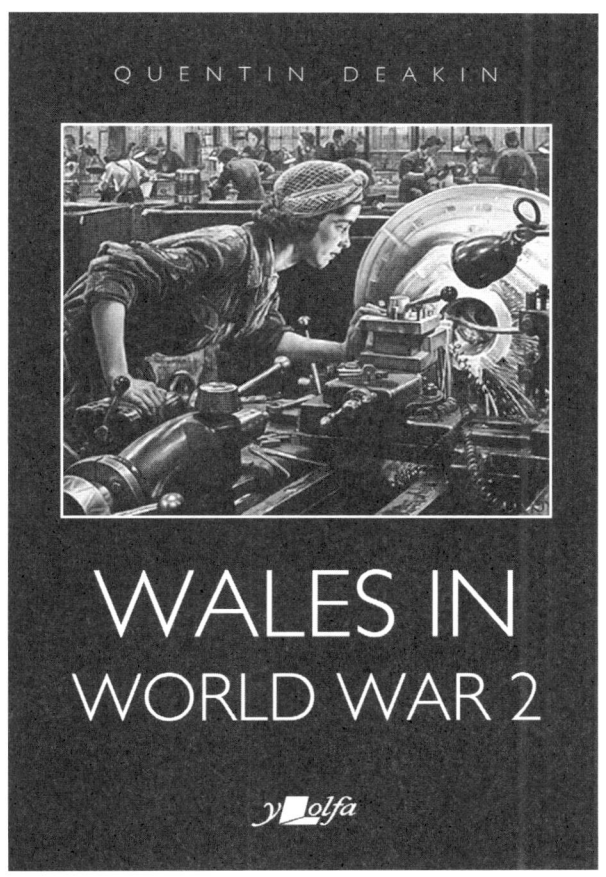

QUENTIN DEAKIN

WALES IN
WORLD WAR 2

y Lolfa

£14.99

A comprehensive account of the part played by Wales in
WW2 and the conflict's impact on every area of the country
and all involved: civilians, factory workers, evacuee children,
politicians, soldiers, pacifists, writers, filmmakers and artists.

M A R T I N   W A D E

On Dragons'
Wings

**A History of No. 614 (County of Glamorgan)
Squadron, Royal Auxiliary Air Force**

£14.99

Very readable history of a Welsh reserve squadron, focusing
primarily on operations in World War Two but taking the
reader from 1930s biplanes through Cold War fighter jets to
disbandment in 1957 and relaunch in 2014.

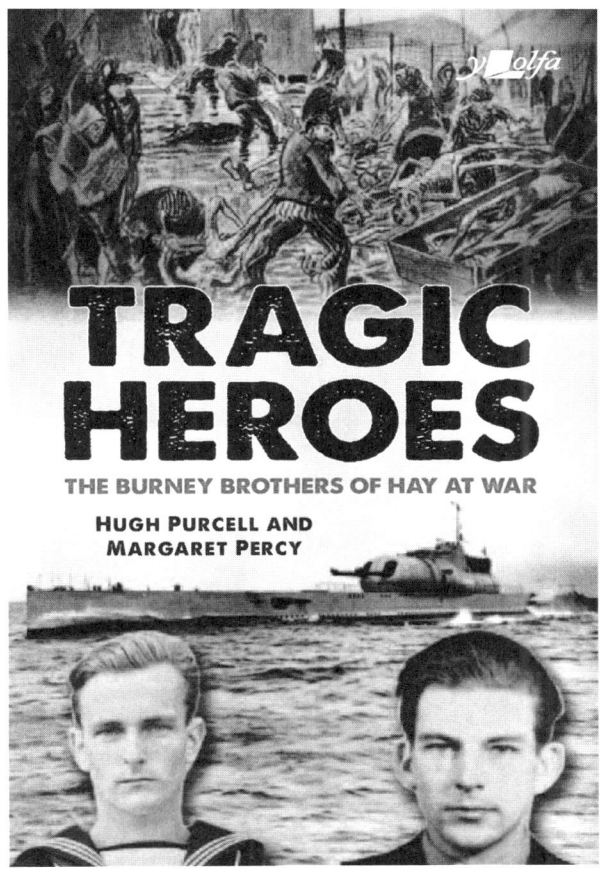

£14.99

The story of two brothers in World War Two.
Christopher Burney was a secret agent tortured by the
Gestapo and sent to a concentration camp, and Roger a
conscientious objector who became a British Naval Liaison
Officer with the Free French, and to whom Benjamin Britten's
'War Requiem' is dedicated.

EVACUEE

FROM THE LIVERPOOL
BLITZ TO WALES

Barbara Warlow Davies

£7.99

The remarkable story of Barbara Warlow Davies, an English-
speaking 4-year-old who was evacuated from Liverpool to
Talgarreg in Ceredigion during the Second World War.

£6.95

The reminiscences of a soldier who fought with
the Welsh Guards during the Second World War.

**Paperback version of *The Auschwitz Goalkeeper*,
Ron Jones' autobiography, coming soon!**